ASIAN POLITICAL, ECONOMIC AND SECURITY ISSUES

BANGLADESH

CONDITIONS, ISSUES AND U.S. RELATIONS

ASIAN POLITICAL, ECONOMIC AND SECURITY ISSUES

Additional books in this series can be found on Nova's website under the Series tab.

Additional e-books in this series can be found on Nova's website under the e-book tab.

ASIAN POLITICAL, ECONOMIC AND SECURITY ISSUES

BANGLADESH

CONDITIONS, ISSUES AND U.S. RELATIONS

GREGORY P. DAVIS
EDITOR

NOVINKA

New York

For permission to use material from this book please contact us:
Telephone 631-231-7269; Fax 631-231-8175
Web Site: http://www.novapublishers.com

Library of Congress Cataloging-in-Publication Data

ISBN: 978-1-63117-003-4

Published by Nova Science Publishers, Inc. † New York

CONTENTS

Preface		**vii**
Chapter 1	Bangladesh: Political and Strategic Developments and U.S. Interests *Bruce Vaughn*	**1**
Chapter 2	Bangladesh Apparel Factory Collapse: Background in Brief *Mary Jane Bolle*	**23**
Chapter 3	Bangladesh 2012 Human Rights Report *U.S. Department of State*	**39**
Chapter 4	Bangladesh 2012 International Religious Freedom Report *U.S. Department of State, Bureau of Democracy, Human Rights and Labor*	**79**
Chapter 5	2013 Investment Climate Statement: Bangladesh *Bureau of Economic and Business Affairs*	**89**
Index		**109**

PREFACE

Bangladesh (the former East Pakistan) is an Islamic-majority nation in South Asia, bordering the Bay of Bengal, dominated by low-lying riparian zones. It is the world's eighth-largest country in terms of population. U.S. policy toward Bangladesh emphasizes support for political stability and democracy, development, and human rights. The United States offers economic assistance to Bangladesh, and has military-to-military ties that include cooperation in multilateral peacekeeping. Bangladesh is also of interest to the United States for the role it plays in the larger geopolitical dynamics of South Asia. This book focuses on the political and strategic developments and United States interests in Bangladesh; provides a background on the Bangladesh apparel factory collapse; discusses the Bangladesh 2012 human rights report as well as the 2012 international religious freedom report; and ends with the 2012 investment climate statement for Bangladesh.

Chapter 1 – Bangladesh (the former East Pakistan) is an Islamic-majority nation in South Asia, bordering the Bay of Bengal, dominated by low-lying riparian zones. It is the world's eighth-largest country in terms of population, with 164 million people housed in a land mass the size of Iowa. Roughly 80% of Bangladesh's population lives on less than $2 per day. It suffers from high levels of corruption and, at times, a faltering democratic system that has been subject to pressure from the military, though the nation has an established reputation as a largely moderate and democratic majority Muslim country.

U.S. policy toward Bangladesh emphasizes support for political stability and democracy, development, and human rights. The United States has long-standing supportive relations with Bangladesh and views Bangladesh as a moderate voice in the Islamic world. The United States offers economic assistance to Bangladesh, and has military-to-military ties that include cooperation in multilateral peacekeeping. Bangladesh is also of interest to the United States for the role it plays in the larger geopolitical dynamics of South Asia.

Bangladesh has been under threat from a combination of political violence, weak governance, poverty, corruption, and Islamist militancy. There has been concern in the past that influence by Islamist extremists could increase and destabilize the country. Such concerns have abated somewhat in more recent years as Islamist militants have been vigorously pursued by authorities and as Bangladesh has returned to democratic government. That said, experts continue to warn that militants may regroup and present new challenges in Bangladesh despite the significant efforts by the government of Bangladesh against them.

The Bangladesh National Party (BNP) and the Awami League (AL) traditionally have dominated Bangladeshi politics, with the AL in power since January 2009. The AL is led by Prime Minister Sheikh Hasina while the BNP is led by former Prime Minister Khaleda Zia. When in opposition, both parties have sought to regain control of the government through demonstrations, labor strikes, and transport blockades. The current Hasina government came to power with an overwhelming majority in parliament. It has moved forward with a war crimes tribunal to prosecute atrocities from the 1971 war of independence from Pakistan. The Hasina government has also moved to strengthen ties with both India and China. With the help of the army, it successfully suppressed a mutiny by the Bangladesh Rifles, a border guard unit, in February 2009.

Demographic pressure and environmental problems, some likely exacerbated by climate change, are increasingly problems for Bangladesh. A rising population, when combined with limited economic resilience and limits on the extent to which agricultural output can be expanded, could prove to be politically destabilizing in the future. Bangladesh's population increases by approximately 2.2 million each year. This raises urgent questions concerning Bangladesh's future food security. Minority groups in Bangladesh, as well as women's rights and security are threatened due to socio-religious prejudices. Another key concern is worker rights and worker safety. Bangladesh is an important part of global supply chains, particularly in the textile industry, and successive factory disasters there have increased global and U.S. concerns about its labor rights regime.

Chapter 2 – The April 24, 2013, collapse of an eight-story garment factory, called Rana Plaza, in Dhaka, Bangladesh, resulted in the deaths of more than 1,100 workers. It is reportedly now considered the deadliest accident in the history of the apparel industry. Congress has had a long-standing interest in supporting internationally recognized worker rights in developing countries, and the building collapse has raised concerns about worker conditions in Bangladesh.

Rana Plaza was allegedly structurally unsound and poorly maintained for apparel production. Apparel production is generally known as an industry under threat of fire, and one where workers need easy access to rapid escape routes. Issues relating to workers' inability to effectively exercise their rights to organize, bargain collectively, and work in a safe workplace may have contributed to the tragedy. For example, workers reportedly noticed cracks in the building and resisted entering, and were told that if they did not report to their jobs, they would not be paid. The factory collapse brought international focus to those parts of global supply chains that may not meet basic safety and health standards.

The U.S. government supports internationally recognized worker rights through various policies and programs. These include U.S. trade preference programs, free trade agreements, foreign assistance, and Department of Labor initiatives.

Congressional and U.S. efforts in this regard are part of an international worker rights support structure in place to offer technical assistance and support to countries—especially developing countries. Other major parts of this structure include international organizations, such as the International Labor Organization (ILO), founded in 1919; and corporate codes of conduct, which have arisen from a broader movement of corporate social responsibility that gained strength in the 1980s and 1990s.

Early analysis of the causes of the Bangladesh tragedy raises questions about what went wrong and about what can be done to help Bangladesh to improve working conditions at factories. Efforts to make changes in Bangladesh are already underway, and developments on this issue are evolving.

This report provides an overview of the recent tragedy in Bangladesh and the Bangladesh economic environment and culture. It also notes the responses to the tragedy, to date, from Congress, the Administration, the ILO, the Bangladesh government, and the private sector. Finally, it raises some possible issues for Congress.

Chapter 3 – Bangladesh is a parliamentary democracy. Prime Minister Sheikh Hasina led the Awami League (AL) to victory in the 2008 parliamentary elections, which international and domestic observers considered free and fair, although with isolated irregularities and sporadic violence. In most instances security forces reported to civil authorities.

The most significant human rights problems were enforced disappearances, discrimination against marginalized groups, and poor working conditions and labor rights. Suspected extrajudicial killings, disappearances, and kidnappings continued, with human rights groups alleging the involvement of the country's security services. Marginalized groups, particularly Rohingya refugees, indigenous people, and women, suffered from unequal treatment and in some instances violence. Workers continued to face difficulties in forming unions and suffered from poor safety conditions in factories, highlighted by a factory fire on November 24.

Other human rights problems included arbitrary arrests, detentions, and custodial deaths. Weak judicial capacity and resultant lengthy pretrial detentions continued to be problems. Authorities infringed on citizens' privacy rights. There were instances in which the government limited freedom of speech and assembly. Some journalists practiced self-censorship. Politically motivated violence and pervasive official corruption remained problems. Some nongovernmental organizations (NGOs) faced legal and informal restrictions on their activities. Many children were compelled to work, due either to economic necessity or in some instances trafficking. Discrimination against persons with disabilities was a problem, especially for children seeking admittance to public school. Instances of societal violence against religious and ethnic minorities persisted, although many government and civil society leaders claimed these acts had political or economic motivations and should not be attributed only to religious beliefs or affiliations. Child marriage of girls was a problem. Discrimination against persons based on their sexual orientation continued. Workers faced obstacles to engaging in collective bargaining. Child labor, particularly in the informal sector, remained a problem.

Official corruption and related impunity remained problems. Weak regard for the rule of law not only enabled individuals, including government officials, to commit human rights violations with impunity but also prevented citizens from claiming their rights. As in the previous year, the government did not take comprehensive measures to investigate and prosecute cases of security force killings.

Chapter 4 – The constitution and other laws and policies protect religious freedom and, in practice, the government generally respected religious freedom. The trend in the government's respect for religious freedom did not change significantly during the year. The government made limited progress on the long-standing issue of returning "vested property" to Hindus dating from the country's liberation war, and also took steps towards equalizing family law for Hindus through legislating optional marriage registration. The constitution states that Islam is the state religion, but reaffirms the nation is a secular state that "shall ensure equal status and equal right in the practice of the Hindu, Buddhist, Christian, and other religions." The constitution provides for the right to profess, practice, or propagate all religions, subject to law, public order, and morality. Although government officials, including police, were sometimes slow to assist members of minority religious groups who were victims of harassment and violence, there were examples of timely and effective police intervention.

There were reports of societal abuses and discrimination based on religious affiliation, belief, or practice. There were scattered attacks on members of minority religious and ethnic groups, most notably against Buddhists in Ramu in September and October. Most attacks consisted of arson and looting of religious sites and homes. Because many members of minority religious groups also had low economic and social status, they were often seen as having little political recourse. Members of Hindu, Christian, Buddhist, and Ahmadiyya Muslim minority groups experienced harassment and sometimes violence from the Sunni Muslim majority population. The government and many civil society leaders stated that violence against members of minority religious groups normally had political or economic dimensions, and could not be attributed solely to religious belief or affiliation.

In meetings with officials and in public statements, the U.S. embassy encouraged the government to protect the rights of members of minority religious groups. The embassy denounced acts of religious intolerance publicly and privately, and called on the government to ensure due process for all citizens. U.S. development programs in the country supported religious tolerance.

Chapter 5 – With a highly competitive labor force, an entrepreneurial business community and a resilient and steadily growing economy, Bangladesh offers promising opportunities for investment, especially in the energy, power, pharmaceutical, information technology and infrastructure sectors and in labor-intensive industries such as ready made garments and household textiles. The Government of Bangladesh actively seeks foreign investment, particularly in energy, power and infrastructure projects. It offers a range of investment incentives under its industrial policy and export-oriented growth strategy, with few formal distinctions between foreign and domestic private investors.

According to the 2012 World Investment Report, Bangladesh received $ 1.13 billion in foreign direct investment in FY12. This represented a 24% increase from the previous financial year, but a nominal amount compared to the $38.9 billion in foreign investment that the entire South Asia region attracted and the traditionally far larger flows that have driven export-led growth in neighboring East Asia. Bangladesh has made gradual progress in reducing some constraints on investment, but inadequate infrastructure, financial constraints, bureaucratic delays and corruption continue to hinder foreign investment. The lack of effective judiciary or alternative dispute resolution mechanisms impedes the enforcement of contracts and the resolution of business disputes.

The installment of the current elected government in 2009 brought greater stability for investors, who were previously reluctant to pursue projects due to risks that decisions might be reversed during the preceding 2006-2009 period when the country experienced three different governments. The approach of national elections in 2013/2014 has raised concern that political uncertainty may hinder investments as continuing disagreement over the institutional mechanism for elections increases the risk of general strikes and street demonstrations that are disruptive to businesses.

In: Bangladesh
Editor: Gregory P. Davis

ISBN: 978-1-63117-003-4

Chapter 1

BANGLADESH: POLITICAL AND STRATEGIC DEVELOPMENTS AND U.S. INTERESTS*

Bruce Vaughn

SUMMARY

Bangladesh (the former East Pakistan) is an Islamic-majority nation in South Asia, bordering the Bay of Bengal, dominated by low-lying riparian zones. It is the world's eighth-largest country in terms of population, with 164 million people housed in a land mass the size of Iowa. Roughly 80% of Bangladesh's population lives on less than $2 per day. It suffers from high levels of corruption and, at times, a faltering democratic system that has been subject to pressure from the military, though the nation has an established reputation as a largely moderate and democratic majority Muslim country.

U.S. policy toward Bangladesh emphasizes support for political stability and democracy, development, and human rights. The United States has long-standing supportive relations with Bangladesh and views Bangladesh as a moderate voice in the Islamic world. The United States offers economic assistance to Bangladesh, and has military-to-military ties that include cooperation in multilateral peacekeeping. Bangladesh is also of interest to the United States for the role it plays in the larger geopolitical dynamics of South Asia.

---

* This is an edited, reformatted and augmented version of a Congressional Research Service publication, CRS Report for Congress R41194, prepared for Members and Committees of Congress, from www.crs.gov, dated August 14, 2013.

Bangladesh has been under threat from a combination of political violence, weak governance, poverty, corruption, and Islamist militancy. There has been concern in the past that influence by Islamist extremists could increase and destabilize the country. Such concerns have abated somewhat in more recent years as Islamist militants have been vigorously pursued by authorities and as Bangladesh has returned to democratic government. That said, experts continue to warn that militants may regroup and present new challenges in Bangladesh despite the significant efforts by the government of Bangladesh against them.

The Bangladesh National Party (BNP) and the Awami League (AL) traditionally have dominated Bangladeshi politics, with the AL in power since January 2009. The AL is led by Prime Minister Sheikh Hasina while the BNP is led by former Prime Minister Khaleda Zia. When in opposition, both parties have sought to regain control of the government through demonstrations, labor strikes, and transport blockades. The current Hasina government came to power with an overwhelming majority in parliament. It has moved forward with a war crimes tribunal to prosecute atrocities from the 1971 war of independence from Pakistan. The Hasina government has also moved to strengthen ties with both India and China. With the help of the army, it successfully suppressed a mutiny by the Bangladesh Rifles, a border guard unit, in February 2009.

Demographic pressure and environmental problems, some likely exacerbated by climate change, are increasingly problems for Bangladesh. A rising population, when combined with limited economic resilience and limits on the extent to which agricultural output can be expanded, could prove to be politically destabilizing in the future. Bangladesh's population increases by approximately 2.2 million each year. This raises urgent questions concerning Bangladesh's future food security. Minority groups in Bangladesh, as well as women's rights and security are threatened due to socio-religious prejudices. Another key concern is worker rights and worker safety. Bangladesh is an important part of global supply chains, particularly in the textile industry, and successive factory disasters there have increased global and U.S. concerns about its labor rights regime.

OVERVIEW: BANGLADESH

With its strategic regional context and a secular and pluralist democracy as well as its status as a moderate Islamist nation, Bangladesh is important to the United States. Although classified as a low-income nation by the World Bank, Bangladesh is a part of the "Next 11" (N-11); the term issued for nations with the largest population and lowest gross domestic product per capita, and the new emerging economies from the developing world.[1] While the nation's growth potential and attraction to investors depends to an extent on its ability to control corruption, it is part of a group of developing nations which, along with the BRIC nations (Brazil, Russia, India, and China), will hold nearly 70% of the world's total population.[2]

In May 2013, the Office of the Spokesperson of the U.S. Department of State released the Joint Statement of the Second U.S.-Bangladesh Partnership Dialogue, highlighting the importance of the nation's development and governance, its partnership of Bangladesh with U.S. agricultural development programs, the possibility of promoting more renewable energy sources, as well as its importance in security measures, including the "continued collaboration in countering extremism, counterterrorism, security assistance, United Nations peacekeeping operations, and humanitarian assistance."[3]

BANGLADESH-U.S. RELATIONS

U.S. policy toward Bangladesh emphasizes support for political stability and democracy, economic development, liberalized trade and investment, human rights, and some military-tomilitary exchange. The United States has long-standing supportive relations with Bangladesh and views Bangladesh as a moderate voice in the Islamic world. The U.S. Department of Defense's Pacific Command works closely with Bangladesh to help expand and improve Bangladesh's peacekeeping, humanitarian assistance, disaster relief, and maritime security capabilities. Bangladesh is viewed by the United States as an important regional actor. The U.S. encourages Bangladesh to allow the "free movement of ideas, goods, and people" and to enhance "regional peace and prosperity."[4]

The State Department views U.S. assistance as vital to strengthening the country following its return to a democratically elected government in 2008. The Obama Administration's Foreign Operations budget request for the 2014 fiscal year seeks to support long-term development in Bangladesh by "addressing the underlying social, demographic, and economic factors that inhibit economic growth and increase vulnerability to extremism." Due to the moderate form of Islamic belief that is prevalent in Bangladesh, the country is valued for its "strong secular and democratic heritage." Bangladesh is a contributor to international security and is valued for its efforts in "countering violent extremism, assisting international peacekeeping, and improving regional connectivity."[5] Bangladesh and the United States have a common interest in working to counter extremist Islamists and their ideology.

Dhaka is a very active participant in international peace operations. Bangladesh has traditionally been and continues to be one of the largest contributors of military and police contingents to United Nations Peace Operations. As of May 2013, 8,836 U.N. police, peacekeeping troops, and U.N. military experts were contributed to United Nations peacekeeping missions.[6]

Bangladesh is situated at the northern extreme of the Bay of Bengal and could potentially be a state of increasing interest in the evolving strategic dynamics between India and China. This importance could be accentuated by the development of Bangladesh's energy reserves and by regional energy and trade routes to China and India. China has become one of Bangladesh's key suppliers of military equipment.[7] At the same time, Bangladesh seeks closer ties and greater cooperation on a range of issues with India.

The May 2013 Bangladesh-U.S. Partnership Dialogue in Dhaka sought to improve the ties between the two nations through governance programs, economic trade, security cooperation, and regional integration. The United States has promised assistance through USAID and President Obama's Global Health Initiative to improve medical detection of infectious diseases, environmentally sustainable initiatives, and nutritional programs to promote local agriculture and increase consumption. In addition, the United States seeks to increase assistance programs for law enforcement, promote business connections, and to transfer a Coast Guard vessel to the Bangladesh Navy. Moreover, U.S. representatives "participated in a roundtable discussion with government, labor, owners and buyers on labor issues in the garment sector."[8]

Workers' Rights and U.S. Policy

Workers' rights have long been a concern in Bangladesh, and U.S. attention on the issue was greatly heightened with the collapse of a Bangladesh factory that produced garments for consumers in the United States and Europe on April 24, 2013, resulting in the deaths of more than 1,100 workers.[9] The accident is considered the deadliest accident in the history of the apparel industry.[10]

The United States has provided Bangladesh with relief from tariffs in the past, under the World Trade Organization's Generalized System of Preferences, to generate trade and economic cooperation in economically emerging nations. These trade privileges for Bangladesh were suspended in June 2013, in the aftermath of the factory disaster, due to concern about labor rights violations in Bangladesh. The goal of the suspension was to encourage Dhaka's actions towards the improvement of labor rights.[11] On July 10, 2013, North American retailers introduced a five-year plan through the Alliance for Bangladesh Worker Safety, which focuses on annual inspections of 500 Bangladeshi factories. It includes 17 retailers and apparel companies including J.C. Penney Co., GAP Inc., Target, and Wal-Mart. The plan, which has raised $42 million as of July 2013, will run on company contributions. It is projected that companies will contribute up to $1 million a year for five years based on how much they produce in Bangladesh.[12] In addition:

> Ten percent of the funds will be set aside to assist workers temporarily displaced by factory improvements or if a factory closes for safety reasons. The money will also support a nongovernmental organization to be chosen within 30 days that will implement parts of the program.[13]

The accord seeks to address factory inspections and safety commitments; common safety standards for factories; worker training; the incorporation of worker's voices through anonymous hotlines; a governing body for the alliance; semi-annual progress reports; support for improvement of factories; and increased involvement with the Bangladeshi government, through local industry groups and worker rights organizations.[14] The plan has been met with criticism by workers' rights groups that note that without the involvement of Bangladeshi workers, and without legal consequences for participating companies, the project cannot succeed.

U.S. Foreign Assistance

The State Department 2014 Budget Justification Document discusses U.S. assistance to Bangladesh by both account and objective. The accounts are specified in *Table 1* below. Additional U.S. assistance for Bangladesh could be in the area of the environment and climate change adaptation and mitigation assistance, as the consequences of climate change for this low-lying nation may increase dramatically in the years ahead. (See "Environmental Concerns, Climate Change, and Food Security" section below.) The U.S. Agency for International Development (USAID) is working with Bangladesh on a multi-stakeholder approach that uses a co-management model to link management authorities and local communities to achieve sustainable natural resource management and biodiversity conservation. Two USAID pilot projects have been carried out. These projects focused on the Management of Aquatic Ecosystems Through Community Husbandry and the Co-Management of Tropical Forest Resources. Under provisions in the U.S. Tropical Forest Conservation Act, the government of Bangladesh and the U.S. government have agreed to pursue a debt-for-nature swap to promote tropical forest conservation in Bangladesh.[15]

Table 1. U.S. Foreign Assistance to Bangladesh by Account and Fiscal Year ($s in thousands)

	FY2012 Actual	FY2014 Request
Development Assistance	81,686	80,900
Foreign Military Financing	2,200	2,500
Global Health Programs (USAID)	71,600	75,300
International Military Education & Training	994	1,000
International Narcotics Control & Law Enforcement	1,394	2,600
Nonproliferation, Antiterrorism, Demining and related Programs	3,666	3,350
Total	204,381	165,650

Source: U.S. State Department, "Bangladesh," Budget Justification Foreign Operations, Annex: Regional Perspectives, 2014, http://www.state.gov/documents/organization/208291.pdf.

A majority of U.S. infrastructure and development assistance in Bangladesh through USAID focuses on health programs. USAID devoted $10 million in assistance in both FY2011 and FY2012 to HIV/AIDS prevention, family planning, child nutrition, and assistance for tuberculosis. USAID prioritizes care for women and children, whose health status is particularly poor.[16]

Domestic Politics, Political Parties, and Elections

Bangladesh is a parliamentary democracy that has traditionally been led by one of two political parties, the Bangladesh National Party (BNP) and the

Awami League (AL). The AL has led the government since January 2009. The AL is led by current Prime Minister Sheikh Hasina while the BNP is led by former Prime Minister Khaleda Zia. When in opposition, both parties have sought to regain control of the government through transport blockades, demonstrations, and general protests and strikes also known as *Hartals*. In June 2011, the opposition BNP Party initiated a *Hartal* to protest government plans to revise the caretaker government provision (see below).

Political violence has long been part of the political landscape in Bangladesh. In 2004-2005, a particularly intensive set of bombings carried out by militants raised questions about political stability. Since that time Bangladesh has done much to curb militant Islamist activity.

The Awami League won an overwhelming electoral victory in the 2008 election and captured 229 of 300 parliamentary seats in Bangladesh's unicameral legislature. The BNP captured only 31 seats in 2008. The AL is the lead party in the Grand Alliance that includes 14 other political parties. The AL does not require their support to govern for its full five-year term of office. The next parliamentary elections must be held by April 2014.[17]

HUMAN RIGHTS

As a low-income nation, Bangladesh argues that it has the right to deny entry to refugees from Burma, which has raised major concerns in the international community. The nation is also accused of unequal rights to women, human trafficking, as well as the lack of attention to violence against minority groups.

The U.S. Department of State 2012 Human Rights Report[18] details that "the most significant human rights problems were enforced disappearances, discrimination against marginalized groups, and poor working conditions and labor rights." Discrimination of women and indigenous people as well as extrajudicial deaths have been raised as points of concern by Human Rights groups. The Human Rights Report also found that, "As in the previous year, the government did not take comprehensive measures to investigate and prosecute cases of security force killings." Furthermore, it found that, "Weak regard for the rule of law not only enabled individuals, including government officials, to commit human rights violations with impunity but also prevented citizens from claiming their rights."[19]

Human Rights Watch notes that Bangladesh's human rights violations increased in 2012, as the government ignored the need "to reform laws and procedures in flawed war crimes and mutiny trials" and protected security forces that remain unprosecuted for human rights violations. The group notes, "Civil society and human rights defenders reported increased governmental pressure and monitoring."[20]

Human rights were further aggravated in 2012 and 2013 by Bangladesh's denial of Burmese refugees, from an Islamic ethnic group, the Rohingya, whose member sought refuge from violence within Burma. The ethnic group was blocked from entry, and denied humanitarian assistance, and protection. An estimated 200,000 Rohingya refugees currently live in Bangladesh, many of whom are unregistered by the government.

Bangladesh suffers from high rates of human trafficking, though government officials are attempting to curb the number of exploited people through a committee created in 2011 that seeks to monitor and prevent human trafficking. As of 2013, Bangladesh stands at a Tier 2 level of the U.S. Department of State's Trafficking in Persons Report.[21] According the U.S. Department of State, "Girls and boys as young as eight years old are subjected to forced prostitution within the country, living in slave-like conditions in secluded environments. Trafficking within the country often occurs from poorer, more rural regions, to cities.[22]" Many of the children are sold into prostitution due to poverty or are introduced into the system by fraud. Recruitment fraud of Bangladeshi immigrants into the Gulf region has proved particularly challenging, while the majority of trafficked women and children, sexually exploited workers and forced laborers are sent to Pakistan and India. Although the Ministry of Home Affairs established a National Plan of Action for Combating Human Trafficking in January 2012, the government has been ineffective in properly curbing human trafficking.[23]

Two political leaders from the BNP and five from the Jamaat-i-Islami have been arrested under the International Crimes (Tribunals) Act and accused of war crimes dating back to Bangladesh's war of secession and independence from Pakistan in 1971.[24] The BNP and Jamaat have opposed the ongoing trials and view them as a move that can help the AL further consolidate its political advantage. As many as three million people were killed and 10 million displaced during the 1971 war that was fought between independence forces in then-East Pakistan, with assistance from India, and the Pakistani army that was largely composed of troops from then West Pakistan. The trials are aimed at those in Bangladesh who allegedly committed war crimes, many of whom are thought to have supported West Pakistan against the Bengali nationalists. Suspects include leading members of the Jamaat-i-Islami Party, the largest Islamist political party in Bangladesh. Jamaat had a paramilitary wing, Al-

Badr, which collaborated with the West Pakistani military during the war for independence and is thought to have assassinated journalists and academics sympathetic to Bengali independence.[25]

Bangladesh has struggled to stabilize relations between Islamist extremists and its minority religious populations, especially Hindus and Buddhists. While Muslim clerics express their condolences and the aberration against Islam that the attacks represent, the religious minorities in the area have faced persecution since independence. The violence against these communities, especially during the war in 1971, have led to mass movements of victims to India and a drop of the Hindu population from 30% of Bangladesh's population in 1947 to 10% today.[26]

Attacks on Buddhist populations in the Chittagong District have continued for years, worrying Sri Lankan communities in the region as well as the Sri Lankan government.[27] Other minority religions that have been discriminated against include Judaism, which has been targeted in the media, and the Ahmadiyya Muslim community.[28]

WOMEN IN BANGLADESH

Many Members of Congress have an interest in promoting women's issues through American development assistance programs including those in Bangladesh. Bangladesh ranks poorly in standards used to judge the rights, abilities, and living standards of women worldwide. For example, in 2012, the UNDP ranked Bangladesh 81st out of 93 countries on the Gender Empowerment Index, a ranking determined by the number of parliament seats held by women, female professionals, technical workers, and senior officials, as well as the female to male ratio in the nation.[29] The Global Gender Gap Index of 2012, a measure created by the World Economic Forum based on measures of economic participation and opportunity, educational attainment, health and survival, and political empowerment factors, placed Bangladesh at 86th out of 135 nations.[30] Nevertheless, Bangladesh has remained relatively better than some other Islamic nations, including Pakistan, which ranked 134th out of 135.

For many poor Bangladeshi women with limited education, the booming textile market of the nation has provided opportunity to work. Nearly 3.6 million women (about 80% of the entire industry[31]) work in Bangladesh's garment industry as of 2013,[32] which, according the UNDP, is "a way out of rural poverty for thousands of Bangladeshi women, as is the case in many other parts of the developing world."[33] A source reports that garment factories remain the most dominant employment opportunity for women, noting that "A World Bank study found in 2008 that compared with other countries, agriculture does not employ as many women in Bangladesh. World Bank experts say this is because land-holding size and agricultural productivity have been historically low, leading to low demand for labour."[34]

In light of the April 2013 garment factory tragedy, Bangladesh and Western governments hope to collaborate on effective reforms for the safety and labor standards for workers in garment factories. The nation is calling on Western investors of the garment industry to ensure that wages are improved from their current $38 per month fare—one of the worst rates in Asia—and to ensure the structural qualities of the factories. Bangladeshi activists as well as development experts note that an improvement in the textile industry and its millions of female workers, would spur Bangladesh's development, through women's tendency to invest steady incomes on the nutrition, education, and healthcare of their families.[35]The garment industry remains an option to avoid the physical toil of agriculture, or as construction workers or house maids.[36]

The increased employment in new textile and garment industries has both created the opportunity for empowerment and heightened social tensions in Bangladesh. *The Guardian* notes that, "While the garment industry has benefited from the cheap labor offered by women—who tend to work for less than men—the industry has reduced the marginalisation of women who were excluded from formal sector jobs."[37] Although providing a route out of poverty to many Bangladeshi women, the right of a female to work without the accompaniment of a male guardian is often questioned by religious fundamentalist in the Islamic-majority nation. Although they provide a large portion of Bangladesh's remittances, women also suffer from vulnerability to abuse and health risks through undocumented migration to the Persian Gulf, India, and other centers of work.[38]

Several international and non-governmental organizations are actively involved in reversing the harmful effects of undocumented migration and empowering Bangladeshi women, including the U.N. Women Bangladesh Program Office's Regional Program to Empower Women Migrant Workers in Asia. USAID also remains an active participant in Bangladesh's struggle for women's equality. The agency notes, "Gender inequity is a cross-cutting issue that affects the long-term development of Bangladesh and hinders economic growth." USAID hopes to incorporate recommendations in projects to increase gender participation; require partners of the organization to develop exercises related to gender parity; have a gender advisor for all project considerations; and assess programs based on gender equity goals.[39]

THE BANGLADESH MILITARY

Bangladesh has suffered through multiple coups and often tense relations between the military and successive civilian governments, since its independence in 1971. Although a parliamentary democracy, since 1990, it "has seen two presidents killed in military coups and 19 other failed coup attempts," which have included the deaths of Hasina's father, Sheikh Mujibur Rahman as well as her opposition, Khaleda Zia's husband, Ziaur Rahman.[40]

Tensions between the military and the government over corruption, poor pay, and poor benefits led members of a paramilitary unit to mutiny on February 25, 2009, and kill 57 officers and 15 of their family members. The two-day mutiny was quickly suppressed by the army.[41] Army Chief of Staff General Muhammad Abdul Mubeen supported Prime Minister Hasina during the mutiny.[42]

More recently, a government deal with Russia has provided the Bangladeshi military with additional arms. After bilateral talks in January 2013, Russia agreed to grant $1 billion in loans for arms purchases to improve military and technical cooperation between the nations. This deal was in addition to Russian grants to Bangladesh's nuclear power plant construction, which currently remains in the initial stages of the project.[43]

ISLAMIST EXTREMISM

Bangladesh was originally founded on secular-socialist principles and grounded in an ethnic Bengali nationalism as opposed to a Muslim religious identity. Some have attributed the rise of Islamist influence in Bangladesh to the failure of Bangladeshi political elites to effectively govern or to provide moral leadership and effectively represent the interests of the masses.[44] Some believe this created political space for the Islamists to gain influence during the previous BNP government.

The U.S. Department of State notes that

> The Government of Bangladesh has demonstrated its commitment to combating domestic and transnational terrorist groups, and its

counterterrorism efforts made it harder for transnational terrorists to operate in or establish safe havens in Bangladesh.[45]

The United States offers assistance to Bangladesh for counterterrorism prevention, monitoring and detection.[46]

Extremist Groups

Several militant extremist groups have operated in Bangladesh, including Jamaat-e-Islami, a group with known connections to Al Qaeda. Other radical groups include Harkat-ul-Jihad-alIslami (HuJI) and the Islamic Oikya Jote, both of which have some international linkages.[47] While Bangladesh has suffered a number of terrorist attacks in the last decade, the government is taking serious steps to curb extremist groups.

The struggle between radicalism and moderate Islam played out in early 2013, when protestors took to the streets of Dhaka in mass numbers to oppose the Hefajat-e-Islam (Protectorate of Islam), an Islamist group, and the government petition to enforce the death penalty on those who blasphemed Islam.[48] The radical Islamist measures seek to punish those who allowed men and women to mix freely and foreign influences,[49] to enforce a mandatory Islamic education and to reinstate religious aspects in the secular nation's constitution. The conflict claimed at least 150 lives by May 2013. CNN reported that "What is happening in Bangladesh is a push and pull between two forces to determine the future direction of the country";[50] it is a struggle between Bangladeshi youths, inspired by social media sources to moderate Islamic fundamentalism in the nation, and Islamic radicals who criticize protestors as anti-Islamic atheists.

U.S. Counterterrorism Efforts in Bangladesh

The United States assists with Bangladesh and other South Asian nations' counterterrorism efforts through military training assistance.[51] The United States' assistance has been especially important for disaster response, terrorism prevention, and to contain radical terrorist groups.

The Government of Bangladesh has also attempted to curb terrorism in recent years through social measures that especially focus on the youth. According to the Country Reports on Terrorism published by the United States

Department of State Bureau of Counterterrorism, "The Ministry of Education provides oversight for madrassas and is developing a standard national curriculum that includes language, math, and science curricula; and minimum standards of secular subjects to be taught in all primary schools, up to the eighth grade," and the "Ministry of Religious Affairs and the National Committee on Militancy Resistance and Prevention work with imams and religious scholars to build public awareness against terrorism."[52] The government has additionally focused on economically empowering women to "buffer against violent extremist messages of male religious leaders."[53]

The Bureau of Democracy, Human Rights, and Labor reports that "The U.S. government offered programs to madrassah students and teachers on religious tolerance, human rights, and gender equality, among other topics. The embassy reached out to influential leaders nationwide, including religious leaders, to introduce the concepts and practices of modern development and democracy through training."[54] USAID and the Bangladesh Ministry of Religious Affairs, as well as the Islamic Foundation, have also cooperated to create a Leaders of Influence (LOI) project in 2011 for Bangladesh which is, in part, used to train Muslim leaders, imams, and other religious leaders of the necessity to promote democracy, tolerance, family planning and social harmony.[55]

Bangladesh in a Regional Context

Bangladesh is a nation of strategic importance not only to the South Asian sub-region but to the larger geopolitical dynamics of Asia as a whole. The Bengalis' struggle with West Pakistan was at the center of the 1971 Indo-Pakistan war. The creation of the independent state of Bangladesh at that time forever weakened Pakistan's position relative to India. This has enabled India to operate as a key actor not only in South Asia, but in Asia as a whole. As a result, in the view of many, India could potentially challenge and/or balance China's emerging strategic posture in Asia. In this way, Bangladesh has played, and will likely continue to play, a role in the shifting regional balance of power between India and China. Some Bangladeshi strategic thinkers believe that the nation should pursue closer ties to China as a strategic counterweight to Bangladesh's relationship with India. The 2010 opening of road and rail routes through Chittagong and Mangla ports in Bangladesh to India's northeast has led others in Bangladesh to talk of developing trade linkages to China.[56] The opening of Burma holds the prospect of further connectivity with the members of the Association of Southeast Asian Nations (ASEAN).

Bangladesh-China Relations

Prime Minister Hasina traveled to China in March 2010 to seek closer cooperation with China in a number of areas. These include Chinese cooperation to construct a deep sea port at Chittagong and to establish a road link from Chittagong to Kunming, China. Some have also called for Chinese investment in developing a deep seaport at Sonadia, which is relatively close to Bangladesh's border with Burma, and using Kunming-Burma road linkages.[57] China reiterated its support for the Deep Sea Port in Chittagong in June 2011.

A "Closer Comprehensive Partnership of Cooperation" joint statement was issued on March 19, 2010, to take bilateral relations between China and Bangladesh forward. The statement called for intensifying cooperation in a number of areas that include sharing hydrological information on the Brahmaputra, intensifying exchanges, Chinese dredging of river beds, enhancing transportation links, increasing bilateral trade, and strengthening exchange and cooperation between the two states' militaries "to safeguard respective national security and stability and promote peace and stability in the region." Bangladesh has reaffirmed its One China policy and expressed support for China's efforts to enhance its cooperation with South Asian Association of Regional Cooperation (SARC) countries.[58]

One issue that bedevils Sino-Bangladesh ties is China's hydropower plans on rivers that flow into South Asia—concerns that are particularly acute in low-lying Bangladesh. China announced plans in 2010 to build a massive dam on the Yarlung Tsangpo River on the upper reaches of the Brahmaputra River. Observers in Bangladesh are concerned about the impact that this and other possible dams may have on the flow of the Brahmaputra including the possible diversion of its flow within China.[59] Ongoing engagement by China with South Asian states, particularly in the area of developing port access, has led to suspicion of China's motives among some in strategic circles in India and the United States. From this perspective, port development in Bangladesh could be seen as part of a "string of pearls" strategy that could in the future be used by China to secure sea lanes that cross the Indian Ocean and link its industrialized eastern seaboard with the energy resources of the Middle East.

China has been developing ports in Gwadar, Pakistan, and at Hambantota, Sri Lanka.

Bangladesh-India Relations

Prime Minister Hasina has pursued improved relations with India as well as with China. India supported Bangladesh's struggle for independence from West Pakistan, of which Bangladesh was a part from 1947 to 1971. As one source points out, "The improved relations are largely due to her efforts to stamp out anti-Indian sentiment in Bangladesh."[60] Despite this, relations between India and Bangladesh have been strained at times due to border disputes, the presence of Islamist militants in Bangladesh, and Indian concern that insurgents from India's northeast have sought refuge inside Bangladesh.

In September 2011, representatives from India and Bangladesh met to draft an agreement for economic and social cooperation and long-term peace and understanding titled "Framework Agreement on Cooperation for Development."[61] Some observers believe the framework is intended to "neutralize China's growing influence" in Bangladesh by providing "more economic leverage to Bangladesh and allow Bangladesh to have a bigger share of India's growing economic success."[62] The agreement addresses many points of contention between the nations including deportment of terrorists harbored in nations, as well as Bangladesh's illegal immigrants and the status of migrant workers. In addition, it promises disaster management aid, scientific, educational, and cultural cooperation between the two nations, environmental protection measures, shared water resources and ties with India's $1 billion pledge in investments for Bangladesh's infrastructure.[63]

Bangladesh has also joined in Indian plans in sharing a hydro-power project in northeastern India. Bangladesh hopes to "obtain a meaningful portion of the power so produced (whether jointly or otherwise"[64] through this deal. The World Bank reports that more than 60% of people do not have access to electricity in Bangladesh.[65]

ECONOMIC DEVELOPMENT AND TRADE

Although it remains one of the world's poorest nations, Bangladesh has experienced consistently sound rates of GDP growth over the past decade. Manufacturing, particularly of readymade garments, and remittances remain key aspects of the Bangladesh economy. Per capita GDP has grown due to economic expansion and slower rates of population growth. GDP almost tripled from 1994 to 2010 while per capita income rose from $325 in 1998 to $588 in 2011. Bangladesh's GDP is generally expected to grow by about 6% in 2013.[66] Despite these achievements much more will have to be done to continue to accommodate the increasing numbers of Bangladeshis entering the workforce.

Bangladesh-U.S. trade has been expanding in recent years, and the United States is Bangladesh's largest trading partner. Although the two nations have discussed a Trade and Investment Framework Agreement (TIFA), Bangladeshi concerns over environmental, labor, and intellectual property provisions have made it reluctant to move forward with a TIFA. American trade and investment interests in Bangladesh include developing natural gas reserves thought to be found in the Bay of Bengal off Bangladesh's coast.

Bangladesh is highly dependent on remittances from Bangladeshis working overseas, which account for 12% of GNP.[67] Two-thirds of Bangladesh revenue from remittances comes from the Middle East. There are an estimated six million Bangladeshis working abroad. They make Bangladesh one of the world's largest sources of overseas workers.[68] Bangladesh textile exports, which are another source of foreign exchange, are reportedly doing well, which may in part offset remittances shortfalls.[69]

In January 2013, Bangladesh revoked its request for financing from the World Bank, objecting to conditions placed on the package, and opted to instead to seek some financial assistance from Russia, which loaned $500 million to Bangladesh for its nuclear power program.

Environmental Concerns, Climate Change, and Food Security

Bangladesh is one of the countries of the world thought most likely to suffer the adverse effects of climate change. Some view it as the most vulnerable country to the negative impact of climate change, due to its low-lying geography.[70]

Demographic pressure and environmental problems, including those linked to climate change, are increasingly problems for Bangladesh as well. The low-lying nation would be significantly affected by projected sea level rise. Some projections are now estimating that, at "the present rate of 8mm a year it may only take about 25 years to raise levels 20cm, enough to permanently waterlog and destroy the land and drinking water of as many as

10 million people in the south of the country."[71] Increasing temperatures during growing seasons in key food exporting nations globally have reduced potential yields and contributed to rising prices.[72] Threats to food production come at a time when global population is projected to increase to 9 billion by 2050. Such climate-related challenges as well as an increasing population, when combined with poor economic resources and limits on the extent to which agricultural output can be expanded, could prove to be politically destabilizing in the future.[73]

Rising sea levels and increased salinity in low-lying areas are thought to be responsible for undermining forest health and leading to lower crop yields. The Intergovernmental Panel on Climate Change (IPCC) has projected that rice and wheat production in Bangladesh could decrease by 8% and 32% respectively by the year 2050 and that rice yields will likely decrease by 10% for every one degree Celsius rise in growing-season minimum temperature.[74] A World Bank Report notes that Bangladesh remains a potential impact hotspot, due to climate change, with more severe river floods, tropical cyclones as well as rising sea levels and high temperatures expected in the future.[75]

Bangladesh reached food self-sufficiency in the 1990s due largely to the introduction of "green revolution" technologies and higher-yielding varieties of rice.[76] Despite this, Bangladesh imports rice, though it is decreasing its rate of importation substantially. In 2012's outgoing fiscal year, Bangladesh's imports of rice and wheat dropped to 2.24 million tonnes from 5.15 million tonnes in 2011.[77]

Bangladesh's lack of resources to accommodate those displaced by environmental changes, and already stressed conditions due to extreme population density, could lead to further cross-border migrations into bordering India, which could exacerbate existing border tensions.

Due to the severe consequences and environmental degradation of Bangladesh, both the international community and the regional governments have sought to reduce the impact of climate change in recent years.[78] While the nation promised to significantly comply, and improve measures to ensure environmental sustainability, it cautions that, "given its resource limitations, the country needs finance and technology transfer as well as capacity enhancement support, consistent with the properly defined tasks that it will take to move steadfastly towards the goal of sustainable development."[79]

USAID is also an active participant in environmental conservation in Bangladesh. In a 2008 Integrated Project Area Co-management (IPAC) project, a five-year investment of $13 million was made to "promote and institutionalize an integrated Protected Area (PA) co-management system for sustainable natural resources management and biodiversity conservation that results in responsible, equitable economic growth and good environmental governance."[80] The organization also accepts that it will adjust its policy towards Bangladesh based on immediate needs, and to cater to long-term goals.

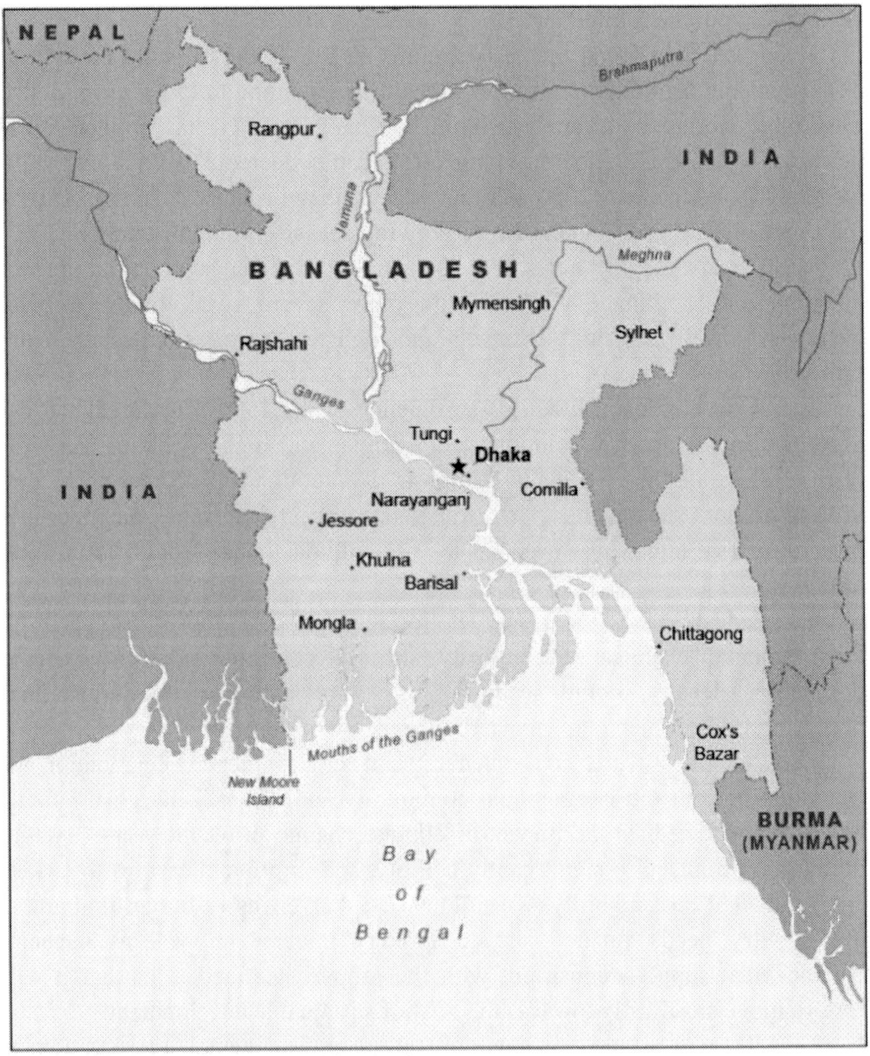

Source: Map Resources Adapted by CRS.

Figure 1. Map of Bangladesh.

End Notes

[1] Deen, M.J., "Looking Beyond the BRICs: Jim O'Neill's 'Next 11,'" Financial Post Business, March 20, 2012.

[2] Ibid.

[3] "Joint Statement of the Second U.S.-Bangladesh Partnership Dialogue," U.S. Department of State, May 27, 2013.

[4] Ibid.

[5] "U.S. Relations with Bangladesh," U.S. Department of State, October 26, 2012.

[6] "Troop and Police Contributors. United Nations Peacekeeping." U.N. News Center, United Nations, May 2013.

[7] "$1b Defence Deal Sealed," The Daily Star, January 16, 2013.

[8] Office of the Spokesperson, "Second U.S.-Bangladesh Partnership Dialogue," U.S. Department of State, May 27, 2013.

[9] For further information on the garment accident and its aftermath, see CRS Report R43085, Bangladesh Apparel Factory Collapse: Background in Brief, by Mary Jane Bolle.

[10] Ali Manik, Julfikar, "Bangladeshis Burn Factories to Protest Unsafe Conditions," Asia Pacific. The New York Times, April 26, 2013.

[11] Greenhouse, Steven, "U.S. to Suspend Trade Privileges with Bangladesh," The New York Times, June 27, 2013.

[12] Wohl, Jessica, and Doug Palmer, "North American Group Sets Bangladesh Factory Safety Plan," Reuters, July 10, 2013.

[13] Ibid.

[14] Mitchell, George, and Olympia Snowe, "Alliance of Leading Retailers in North America Join Forces in Comprehensive, Five-Year Commitment to Improve Factory Safety Conditions for Workers in Bangladesh," Bipartisan Policy Center, July 10, 2013.

[15] "U.S. AID's Response: Environment," USAID Bangladesh, May 10, 2013.

[16] "U.S. Agency for International Development," Health in Bangladesh.

[17] "Bangladesh: Country Report," The Economist Intelligence Unit, May 2011.

[18] Bureau of Democracy, Human Rights and Labor, State Department, "2012 Human Rights Report: Bangladesh," 2012.

[19] Ibid.

[20] "World Report 2013," Bangladesh, The Human Rights Watch, 2013.

[21] "Trafficking in Persons Report 2013," Bangladesh, U.S. Department of State, 2013.

[22] Ibid.

[23] Ibid.

[24] "Unique Opportunity for Justice for 1971 Atrocities," Human Rights Watch, May 19, 2011.

[25] "Bangladesh Politics: Do Mention the War," The Economist, July 23, 2009.

[26] Ibid.

[27] "Attack on Buddhist Temples in Chittagong—No Cause for Alarm," Ministry of External Affairs, Colombo, Sri Lanka, September 5, 2012.

[28] "International Religious Freedom Report for 2012," Bureau of Democracy, Human Rights and Labor, U.S. Department of State, 2012.

[29] "Gender Empowerment Measure," United Nations Development Programme, 2012.

[30] Hausmann, Ricardo, Laura D. Tyson, and Saadia Zahidi, "The Global Gender Gap Report," World Economic Forum, 2012.

[31] Ibid.

[32] Al-Mahmood, Syed Zain, "Bangladesh's Garment Industry Still Offers Women Best Work Opportunity," The Guardian. Guardian News and Media, May 23, 2013.
[33] Chhibber, Ajay, "Bangladesh Tragedy Exposes Need for Responsible Globalization," United Nations Development Programme, May 28, 2013.
[34] Al-Mahmood, Syed Zain, "Bangladesh's Garment Industry Still Offers Women Best Work Opportunity," The Guardian. Guardian News and Media, May 23 2013.
[35] Pasricha, Anjana, "Bangladesh Hopes Garment Sector Change Will Empower Women," Voice of America. June 5, 2013.
[36] Pasricha, Anjana, "Bangladesh Hopes Garment Sector Change Will Empower Women," Voice of America. June 5, 2013.
[37] Al-Mahmood, Syed Zain, "Bangladesh's Garment Industry Still Offers Women Best Work Opportunity," The Guardian, Guardian News and Media, May 23, 2013.
[38] Al-Mahmood, Syed Zain, "Bangladesh's Women Take Rocky Road to India in Search of Freedom and Cash," The Guardian, Guardian News and Media, January 31, 2013.
[39] "Gender Equality and Women's Empowerment," U.S. Agency for International Development, May 10, 2013.
[40] "Bangladeshi Military 'foils Coup Plot,'" The Guardian, January 19, 2012.
[41] "BDR Peelkhana Mutiny Trial Begins Today," The Daily Star, February 23, 2010.
[42] "Charges for Bangladesh Mutineers," BBC News, March 1, 2009.
[43] "Russia Grants Bangladesh $1 Billion Loan for Weapons: Putin," Reuters U.S., January 15, 2013.
[44] Ali Riaz, God Willing: The Politics of Islamism in Bangladesh (New York: Rowman and Littlefield Publishers, 2004).
[45] U.S. Department of State, "Country Reports: South Asia Overview," in Country Reports on Terrorism, released by the Office of the Coordinator for Counterterrorism, May 2013.
[46] Ibid.
[47] For further information on extremists groups, see CRS Report RS22591, Islamist Extremism in Bangladesh, by Bruce Vaughn.
[48] "Islamist Protests Rock Dhaka," Asia News, May 10, 2013.
[49] "Hard-Line Muslim Rally Demands Anti-Blasphemy Laws in Bangladesh," The New York Times, April 7, 2013.
[50] Ahmed, Saeed, Farid Ahmed, and Sajjad Hussein, "Bangladeshi Capital Wears an Eerie Calm a Day after Islamists Battle Police," CNN, Cable News Network, May 6, 2013.
[51] "Pentagon Commander Says U.S. Special Forces in India," BBC, February 3, 2012.
[52] U.S. Department of State, "Country Reports: South Asia Overview," in Country Reports on Terrorism, released by the Office of the Coordinator for Counterterrorism, May 2013.
[53] U.S. Department of State, "Country Reports: South Asia Overview," in Country Reports on Terrorism, released by the Office of the Coordinator for Counterterrorism, May 2013.
[54] "International Religious Freedom Report for 2012," Bureau of Democracy, Human Rights and Labor, U.S. Department of State, 2012.
[55] U.S. Department of State, "Country Reports: South Asia Overview," in Country Reports on Terrorism, released by the Office of the Coordinator for Counterterrorism, May 2013.
[56] "Dhaka Should Balance Ties with Delhi, Beijing," Plus News Pakistan, March 15, 2010.
[57] "Bangladesh: Balacing Ties with Delhi and Beijing," China Forum, April 13, 2010.
[58] "Dhaka-Beijing Jt Statement Outlines Closer Cooperation," The Daily Star, March 20, 2010.
[59] "Dhaka to Play Diplomacy Card with China," bdnews24.com, June 17, 2011.
[60] Kumar, Sanjay, "India's Growing Ties with Bangladesh," The Pulse Perspectives on South Asia, The Diplomat, February 1, 2013.

[61] "Reconfiguring Bangladesh-India Relations," The Hindu, March 26, 2013.

[62] Kumar, Sanjay, "India's Growing Ties with Bangladesh," The Pulse Perspectives on South Asia, The Diplomat, February 1, 2013.

[63] "Framework Agreement on Cooperation for Development Between Government of the Republic of India and Government of the People's Republic of Bangladesh," September 2011; and Kumar, Sanjay, "India's Growing Ties with Bangladesh," The Pulse Perspectives on South Asia, The Diplomat, February 1, 2013.

[64] "Reconfiguring Bangladesh-India Relations," The Hindu, March 26, 2013.

[65] "The Most Bucks for the Biggest Bang," The Economist, February 6, 2013.

[66] "HSBC Global Connections Report—Bangladesh," HSBC Global Connections, February 2013.

[67] "Remittances Profile: Bangladesh." Migration Policy Institute, 2011.

[68] "Labour Migration." International Labour Organization, 2013.

[69] "The Arab Spring's Chill Winds," The Economist, April 23, 2011.

[70] Devin Hagerty, "Bangladesh in 2007," Asian Survey, February 2008.

[71] Vidal, John, "Sea Change: The Bay of Bengal's Vanishing Islands," The Guardian, Guardian News and Media, January 29, 2013.

[72] Lesley Russell, "Pressure on Food Begins to Bite," Canberra Times, June 10, 2011.

[73] Bangladesh's Census: In Search of Common Denominator," The Economist, March 17, 2011.

[74] IPCC, Climate Change 2007: Working Group II: Impacts, Adaptation and Vulnerability, 2007.

[75] "Warming Climate to Hit South Asia Hard with Extreme Heat, Floods, and Disease, World Bank Report Says," The World Bank, June 19, 2013.

[76] "Is Growth in Bangladesh's Rice Production Sustainable?" http://ideas.repec.org.

[77] Parvez, Sohel, Bangladesh's Food Import Dips by Half, The Daily Star, January 28, 2012.

[78] "Rio + 20: National Report on Sustainable Development," Bangladesh, RIO +, May 20, 2012.

[79] Ibid.

[80] "USAID: Bangladesh: Environment," USAID: Bangladesh: Environment, September 27, 2011.

In: Bangladesh
Editor: Gregory P. Davis

ISBN: 978-1-63117-003-4

Chapter 2

BANGLADESH APPAREL FACTORY COLLAPSE: BACKGROUND IN BRIEF*

Mary Jane Bolle

SUMMARY

The April 24, 2013, collapse of an eight-story garment factory, called Rana Plaza, in Dhaka, Bangladesh, resulted in the deaths of more than 1,100 workers. It is reportedly now considered the deadliest accident in the history of the apparel industry. Congress has had a long-standing interest in supporting internationally recognized worker rights in developing countries, and the building collapse has raised concerns about worker conditions in Bangladesh.

Rana Plaza was allegedly structurally unsound and poorly maintained for apparel production. Apparel production is generally known as an industry under threat of fire, and one where workers need easy access to rapid escape routes. Issues relating to workers' inability to effectively exercise their rights to organize, bargain collectively, and work in a safe workplace may have contributed to the tragedy. For example, workers reportedly noticed cracks in the building and resisted entering, and were told that if they did not report to their jobs, they would not be paid. The factory collapse brought international focus to those

* This is an edited, reformatted and augmented version of a Congressional Research Service publication, CRS Report for Congress R43085, prepared for Members and Committees of Congress, from www.crs.gov, dated June 14, 2013.

parts of global supply chains that may not meet basic safety and health standards.

The U.S. government supports internationally recognized worker rights through various policies and programs. These include U.S. trade preference programs, free trade agreements, foreign assistance, and Department of Labor initiatives.

Congressional and U.S. efforts in this regard are part of an international worker rights support structure in place to offer technical assistance and support to countries—especially developing countries. Other major parts of this structure include international organizations, such as the International Labor Organization (ILO), founded in 1919; and corporate codes of conduct, which have arisen from a broader movement of corporate social responsibility that gained strength in the 1980s and 1990s.

Early analysis of the causes of the Bangladesh tragedy raises questions about what went wrong and about what can be done to help Bangladesh to improve working conditions at factories. Efforts to make changes in Bangladesh are already underway, and developments on this issue are evolving.

This report provides an overview of the recent tragedy in Bangladesh and the Bangladesh economic environment and culture. It also notes the responses to the tragedy, to date, from Congress, the Administration, the ILO, the Bangladesh government, and the private sector. Finally, it raises some possible issues for Congress.

BACKGROUND AND OVERVIEW[1]

On April 24, 2013, Rana Plaza, an eight-story building, in Dhaka, Bangladesh, collapsed, killing more than 1,100 garment workers. It brought international focus on portions of the global supply chain. It also raised the issue of what might be done to improve working conditions, especially for lower-wage workers in developing countries around the world.

According to press reports, the day of the building collapse workers arrived and saw cracks in the outside of the building where five manufacturing operations were trying to meet production deadlines on apparel products for the U.S. and European Union (EU) markets.[2]

Reportedly, management assured them that the building was safe, and told workers that they would not be paid if they did not work. An hour later, the building collapsed. It has been labeled the deadliest disaster in the history of the garment industry.[3]

Source: U.S. Department of State.

Note: Bangladesh, about the size of Iowa, with a population half that of the United States, is tucked into to the eastern end of India; it also borders Burma.

Figure 1. Map of Bangladesh.

The Rana Plaza collapse took place five months after a December 17, 2012, fire at another Bangladesh apparel factory, Tazreen Fashions Limited; the Tazreen fire killed 112 workers.[4] Survivors reportedly stated that their managers locked one exit route and told workers that the fire alarms were false, thereby delaying timely evacuation.[5] The combined tragedies brought the six-month total loss of life in Bangladesh in the garment sector to at least 1,200. After the building collapse, reportedly, thousands of workers took to the streets and vandalized vehicles and shops before being dispersed by police. Soon after that, the government initially shut down 18 apparel factories, for safety reasons, as concerns about industrial safety across the country continued to grow.[6]

Bangladesh's major export is apparel, which, along with a small amount of textiles, accounts for more than 80% of the country's $23 billion in exports to the world in 2011, or nearly $20 billion. (See *Text Box 1.*) As a result of the Rana Plaza building collapse, some firms, such as Disney,[7] have indicated they may no longer source production from Bangladesh, largely due to concerns over their brand reputation. If this becomes a major trend, one consequence could be that many women, who constitute 80% of the workers in the apparel sector, could lose their jobs. These women, mostly Muslim, have found new independence and an increased standard of living for their families, and have, in many cases, become primary breadwinners. The effect on the economic structure of Bangladesh could be compounded by an ongoing struggle between a secular Bangladeshi identity and a more fundamental/religious Islamic identity.[8] A number of factors may have led to the recent building collapse. Bangladesh's economy is labor-intensive, which attracts lower-wage and lower-skilled industries such as apparel. Bangladesh is a densely populated country, where a population half the size of the United States is crowded into a geographic area the size of Iowa. To meet increasing global demand for apparel production, primarily by the United States and Europe, certain buildings may have been converted to multistory manufacturing operations. In many countries, apparel production is generally carried out in one- or two-story buildings because of the inherent fire hazards associated with this production. Three additional floors that reportedly were illegally constructed were added to the Rana Plaza.[9]

According to press reports, working conditions in Bangladesh were theoretically addressed, at least in part, by Bangladesh labor laws and building codes, International Labor Organization (ILO) commitments, codes of conduct held by multinational corporations, and GSP trade preferences.

ILO

Since 1972, Bangladesh has been a member of the International Labor Organization (ILO). The ILO originated in 1919 as a tripartite organization comprised of workers, employers, and governments, to promote "decent work" around the world. Under the 1998 *ILO Declaration on Fundamental Principles and Rights at Work*, Bangladesh and all ILO members have an obligation to uphold ILO core labor principles, simply by reason of their status as ILO members, even if they have not ratified the conventions behind the principles. Bangladesh has, however, ratified seven of the eight ILO conventions backing and defining the five core labor principles.[10] These principles are very similar to the U.S. list of internationally recognized worker rights.

Bangladesh in Brief

History and Government: The United States established diplomatic relations with Bangladesh in 1972, after its independence from Pakistan through a 1971 war. Its government is a parliamentary democracy. The State Department describes relations between the two countries as "excellent," reflecting "strong bonds of friendship and shared values." The CIA *Factbook* describes Bangladesh as being "poor, overpopulated, and inefficiently governed." (Sources: U.S. Department of State, U.S. Relations with Bangladesh, and CIA, *The World Factbook*.)

Geography and Population: Situated on the Ganges River Delta, on the Bay of Bengal, Bangladesh is mostly surrounded by India, and is adjacent to Burma. Bangladesh's population is about 164 million, half that of the United States, crowded into a land mass slightly smaller than Iowa. Its capital is Dhaka, which has a population of about 14 million. (Source: CIA *Factbook*.)

Economy: Challenges to Bangladesh's economy include having "political instability, poor infrastructure, corruption, insufficient power supplies, and slow implementation of economic reforms." In 2012, on a purchasing power parity basis, its GDP was $306 billion, or $2,000 per capita, with nearly one-third of the population living below the poverty line. Its labor force is divided into 45% in agriculture, 30% in industry, and 25% in services. Its average annual GDP growth rate since 1996 is 5.8%. Its most important industries are jute, cotton, and garments. (Source: CIA *Factbook*.)

Trade and Investment: Bangladesh's major export is apparel, which, along with a small amount of textiles, accounts for more than 80% of the country's $23 billion in exports to the world in 2011, or nearly $20 billion. It represents an apparel export total that is fourth in the world, after China. The United States is Bangladesh's largest export market, accounting for nearly 20% of the country's exports in 2011. In 2012, the United States imported $4.9 billion in goods from Bangladesh, of which $4.5 billion or 92% were textiles and apparel. U.S. exports to Bangladesh in 2012 totaled $502 million, led by cotton, machinery, and iron and steel. In 1989, the United States and Bangladesh signed a bilateral investment treaty. World foreign direct investment in Bangladesh currently totals about $7.8 billion. (Source: CIA *Factbook*, Global Trade Atlas, and Department of Commerce, Office of Textiles and Apparel (OTEXA.))

Labor: Bangladesh has a labor force of about 77 million (nearly half of its population), of which about 3.6 million-4.5 million, depending on sources consulted, are apparel workers employed in nearly 4,500 manufacturing operations. Minimum wages are $37 per month. Wages in export processing zones are typically higher. The official unemployment rate is about 5%, but about 40% of the labor force is underemployed. (Sources: State Department: *Country Reports on Human Rights Practices*, 2012, and CIA *Factbook*.)

GSP Status: Bangladesh is listed as a designated "beneficiary developing country" under the Generalized System of Preferences (GSP), and is therefore eligible for U.S. tariff preferences for certain products as long as it meets country eligibility requirements, including worker rights criteria that require a country to have taken or be taking steps to "afford internationally recognized worker rights" to its workers, including any in a designated zone. These core worker rights are defined in Section 507(4) of the Trade Act of 1974 as (a) the right of association; (b) the right to organize and bargain collectively; (c) a prohibition on the use of forced or compulsory labor; (d) a minimum age for the employment of children; and (e) acceptable conditions of workers with respect to minimum wages, hours of work, and occupational safety and health. In 2012, U.S. GSP imports from Bangladesh totaled $35.4 million, out of a total import value of $4.9 billion. Apparel and textile products are largely excluded from GSP tariff-free benefits. (Sources: Harmonized Tariff Schedule of the United States; Trade Act of 1974, P.L. 93-618 as amended, 19 U.S.C. 2461; and U.S. International Trade Commission (USITC) Trade Database.)

ILO Core Labor Principles: In 1972, a year after its independence from Pakistan, Bangladesh ratified six of the eight ILO core labor conventions (discussed elsewhere in this report).

According to the Department of State, the most significant human rights problems in Bangladesh included poor working conditions and poor protection of labor rights. Safety conditions at many workplaces were described as "extremely poor." Enforcement of acceptable conditions for workers was reportedly hindered by a lack of labor inspectors. However, because of high unemployment and inadequate enforcement of laws, workers who demanded redress for dangerous working conditions or who refused to work under hazardous conditions risked losing their jobs (Sources: ILO, and State Department, *Country Reports on Human Rights Practices*, p. 39.)

Brand Names: Brand name products produced in Bangladesh include H&M, C&A, Nike, Reebok, GAP, JCPenney, Walmart, Kmart, Wrangler, Dockers, Tommy Hilfiger, Adidas, Eddie Bauer, Eagle, and American Eagle. (Source: Bangladesh Export Processing Zones Authority.)

These rights are the following:

1) freedom of association and the effective recognition of the right to collective bargaining;
2) the elimination of all forms of forced or compulsory labor;
3) the effective abolition of child labor, including the worst forms of child labor; and
4) the elimination of discrimination in respect of employment and occupation.[11]

Whether countries do or do not uphold ILO core labor principles, the ILO has no real enforcement powers other than technical assistance, reporting requirements, publication of information, and moral suasion. An example of ILO activities to enhance worker rights is the Better Work Program, which is currently in place in Haiti and Cambodia. It is a joint program with the World Bank that works with government officials, factory owners, and labor groups to ensure safe and decent workplace conditions. It does not currently operate in Bangladesh. (See section on ILO response.)

Figure 2, below, shows that the concepts of the ILO core labor principles promoted by the ILO-World Bank Better Work program, plus the ILO occupational safety and health principle, are included as U.S. internationally recognized worker rights, and are incorporated into some private sector codes of conduct. Thus, *Figure 2* shows graphically the extent to which similar sets of rights extend through all three parts of the international worker rights support system.

U.S. Trade Preference Programs[12]

One area of congressional focus in supporting internationally recognized worker rights has been through provisions in U.S. trade preference programs. These were first introduced in the Generalized System of Preferences (GSP) program in 1985.[13] GSP provides unilateral U.S. tariff preferences for certain products exported by developing countries, to support their economic development. Under GSP, and later introduced in other trade preference programs, the President or his designee is prohibited from designating certain countries as eligible for GSP benefits, based on different criteria, including that a country "has not taken or is not taking steps to afford internationally recognized worker rights."[14] These worker rights are defined as

1) the right of association;
2) the right to organize and bargain collectively;
3) a prohibition on the use of any form of forced or compulsory labor;
4) a minimum wage for the employment of children; and protection against the worst forms of child labor;[15] and
5) acceptable conditions of work with respect to minimum wages, hours of work, and occupational safety and health.

Bangladesh is currently a beneficiary country under GSP. If the President determines that Bangladesh is no longer meeting GSP criteria, he may suspend benefits. In 2007, the Office of the U.S. Trade Representative (USTR) first accepted a petition from the AFL-CIO for review of GSP status for Bangladesh. The petition challenged whether Bangladesh was meeting the GSP worker rights criteria. That decision is still pending.[16]

The GSP program, however, excludes from eligibility most apparel and textile articles (and other import sensitive products), which constitute 92% of Bangladesh's exports to the United States. Therefore, if GSP benefits were suspended, the decision would not affect U.S. tariffs on apparel imports, which reportedly average about 16%.[17] On the other hand, some businesses might decide to pull out of Bangladesh for fear that association with a country that has lost its GSP status for reasons relating to internationally recognized worker rights could damage their reputations. Some may argue that suspension of GSP status could significantly reduce Bangladesh's apparel-making labor force and adversely impact its economy.

Corporate Codes of Conduct[18]

Since the 1980s and 1990s, when globalization accelerated and various interest groups began to publicize "bad actors" on worker rights conditions in factories, corporations have increasingly adopted and publicized corporate codes of conduct. Most, if not all, large multinational corporations sourcing apparel from Bangladesh have posted such codes on their websites. These codes may describe the standards to which the business holds its employees, its suppliers under contract, and sometimes its subcontractors. These codes specify worker rights protections and structural and fire hazard standards to varying degrees. A concern raised by some groups is that corporations may contract directly with suppliers, yet have limited knowledge of the conditions under which the products are produced by subcontractors. Corporate codes of conduct are voluntary on the part of corporations. The Rana Plaza collapse has focused greater attention on the worker conditions and laws in Bangladesh, and may impact Bangladesh's continued role as a major supplier of apparel, due to corporate buyer concerns over branding and reputation. Key issues may include whether firms will continue to source apparel from Bangladesh, or whether firms will engage more proactively to improve conditions there, as well as the extent to which corporate codes of conduct have been helpful.[19]

A number of interested parties, including parties in Europe and the United States, among them President Obama, and a number of Members of Congress, are calling for U.S. and European companies and other stakeholders to work together to solve the problems. (See section below.)

U.S. and International Responses to the Bangladesh Tragedy

Response to the Bangladesh tragedy has come from Congress, the Administration, the ILO, the Bangladesh government, and the private sector, and is evolving. This section briefly describes recent developments.

Congress

Some Members of Congress, to date, have focused on seeking businesses and other stakeholders to work together to improve worker conditions in Bangladesh. On May 1, 2013, for example, Representatives Sander Levin, ranking Member of the House Ways and Means Trade Subcommittee, and George Miller, ranking Member of the House Education and the Workforce Committee, sent a letter to President Obama, urging the Administration to convene representatives of European and American retailers, the Bangladesh garment industry (including their workers and unions), the Bangladeshi government, the ILO, and non-governmental organizations, to facilitate development of a "concrete action plan" to address the range of issues relating to working conditions and worker rights in the garment sector.[20]

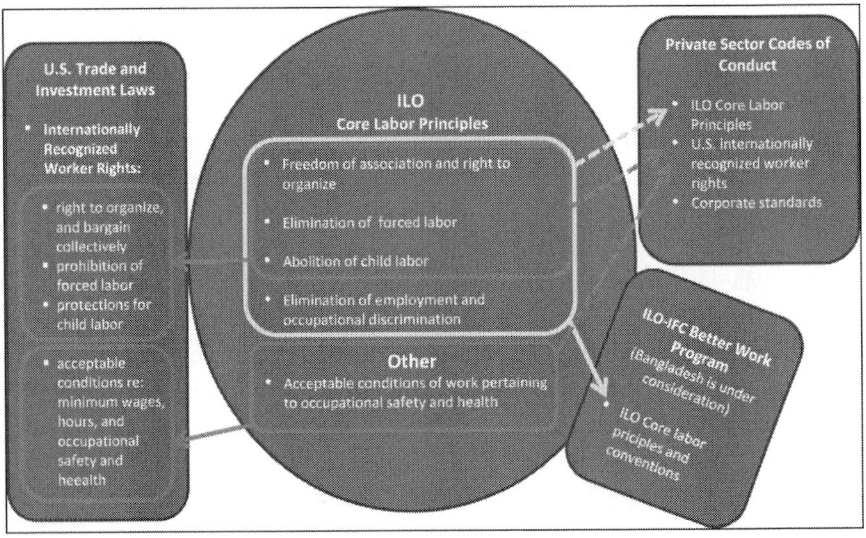

Source: Graphic prepared by CRS.

Figure 2. Worker Rights Principles Included in ILO Core Labor Principles, U.S. Trade Preferences and Agreements, and Some Private Sector Codes of Conduct.

In addition, a group of eight U.S. Senators, led by Senators Harry Reid and Sherrod Brown, has written letters to major retailers that source in Bangladesh, urging them to reconsider signing the legally binding "Accord on Fire and Building Safety in Bangladesh." This Accord has already been signed by a number of U.S. and European retailers. Some U.S. retailers who have not signed have reportedly opted for self-monitoring or voluntary initiatives due to concerns over liability. The companies receiving the letters had previously declined to sign the accord.[21] A House group of 10 Representatives, led by House Minority Leader Nancy Pelosi and House Minority Whip Steny Hoyer, sent a somewhat similar letter to nine of the U.S. retailers who also received the Senate letter.[22] (See further discussion of the Accord under "Private Sector," below.)

Executive Branch

State Department, USTR, and Labor Department Response: On May 8, 2013, the State Department, Department of Labor, and USTR convened a conference call with U.S. buyers in Bangladesh's garment industry. In that call, they "strongly urged" U.S. (corporate) buyers to coordinate efforts with each other, and with the government of Bangladesh, the Bangladesh Garment Manufacturers and Exporters Association (BGNEA), civil society, and labor groups to (a) help pay for independent safety and fire inspectors; (b) communicate to the Bangladeshi government their concerns about labor conditions; and (c) urge immediate passage of labor law amendments to lay the basis for the establishment of an ILO/World Bank Better Work Program for Bangladesh.[23]

On June 13, 2013, the Department of Labor's Bureau of International Labor Affairs (ILAB) announced that a competitive grant of $2.5 million would be awarded to recipient(s) who would work to (1) strengthen the Bangladesh government's ability to improve and enforce fire and building safety standards; and (2) build the capacity of worker organizations to effectively monitor violations of such standards and abate hazards in the ready-made garment sector.[24]

GSP Status for Bangladesh: The USTR is evaluating GSP status for Bangladesh as part of its annual review process. The review was already underway at the time the building collapsed. The USTR had accepted an AFL-CIO petition on Bangladesh that was first submitted in 2007 and then updated in 2012, after the Tazreen fire. The GSP Trade Policy Staff Committee held hearings in March of 2013 on the issue, and its decision on whether to suspend GSP preferences for Bangladesh is pending. In the past, the USTR has suspended GSP status for worker rights issues, including for Burma.

ILO

The ILO acted after the disaster to help Bangladesh focus on what needed to be done. On May 1- 4, shortly after the Rana Plaza building collapse, the ILO sent a delegation led by the Deputy Director General for Field Operations and Partnerships to engage with the tripartite partners and other stakeholders to identify what should be done to prevent future tragedies. They agreed on the need to develop an action plan, focusing on a number of short- and medium-term steps. These include (a) submission to parliament of a labor law reform package; (b) assessment by the end of 2013 of the structural and fire safety status of all export-oriented ready-made garment factories; (c) recruitment of 200 additional factory inspectors within six months; (d) implementation of a National Tripartite Plan of Action on Fire Safety, which also addresses the structural integrity of buildings; and (e) focus on a possible ILO/World Bank Better Work program for Bangladesh, already under consideration.[25] After a nine-month "participatory design phase," which began in 2012, and further assessment of the potential for successful implementation of a Better Work Program for Bangladesh, the ILO-World Bank has declined to permit Bangladesh to join a textile industry monitoring program until the country overhauls its labor laws, and conditions for unions improve.[26] (See "Bangladesh Government" actions below.)

Bangladesh Government

The Bangladesh government response after the tragedy was to begin working with the ILO to focus on changes needed. As a result, the Bangladesh cabinet has reportedly approved some changes to its labor laws—changes that will require approval by the Bangladesh Parliament, scheduled to convene in June. These changes would (1) make it easier for workers to form labor unions; (2) increase severance and retirement payments for workers with longer tenures; and (3) equalize, for all workers, annual payments under a welfare fund. Government officials are also reportedly beginning discussions between labor and management on setting a new minimum wage for garment workers, who are reportedly "increasingly angry" about low wages, particularly in light of recent inflation.[27] In addition, the government reportedly plans to add 200 factory inspectors within six months, and to complete a comprehensive safety assessment (extending to fire and structural safety) of all export-oriented garment factories.[28]

Private Sector

Private sector responses have varied. According to press reports, retailers and some apparel firms have acknowledged their links to unsafe Bangladesh factories, while others have hedged.[29] Another private sector response to the tragedy has been for businesses to debate whether to leave Bangladesh and relocate to countries with fewer high-visibility labor issues, or stay and help solve them in Bangladesh. Some companies, including Disney, as previously mentioned, are considering not sourcing from Bangladesh for a number of reasons, including concerns about their business reputation.[30]

A broader response from many corporations, particularly in Europe, has been to join forces to support change in Bangladesh. After the building collapse, officials from two dozen retailers and apparel companies met with representatives from the German government to try to negotiate a plan to ensure safety at roughly 4,500 garment factories in Bangladesh.[31] On May 13, 2013, several of the world's largest apparel companies reportedly agreed to a legally binding "Accord on Fire and Building Safety in Bangladesh" to help pay for fire safety and building improvements in Bangladesh. The Accord requires a five-year commitment from participating retailers to conduct independent safety inspections of factories, and pay up to $500,000 per year toward safety improvements. European corporations that have signed onto the accord include Swedish retail giant H&M (the largest producer of apparel in Bangladesh); Inditex, headquartered in Spain; C&A, a Dutch retailer; and Primark and Tesco (British retailers). U.S. signatories include PVH, the parent company of Calvin Klein, Tommy Hilfiger, and Izod, which has signed on to the five-year plan, contributing $2.5 million; and Abercrombie and Fitch. [32] A coalition of faith organizations, investors, and labor groups, including the AFL-CIO, is urging major U.S. retailers, including Walmart, Gap, Sears, and others, to sign onto the plan.[33]

Other U.S. companies, including Walmart and Gap, have reportedly resisted signing, objecting to the agreement's legally binding nature, and arguing that they have pursued or are pursuing their own initiatives, such as the hiring of fire inspectors and promising loans for factory improvements.[34] One such initiative is an "action plan" being organized by the Bipartisan Policy Center (BPC), co-chaired by former Senate Majority Leader George Mitchell and former Senator Olympia Snowe. Parties to an alliance supporting this proposed plan include the American Apparel & Footwear Association, National Retail Federation, Retail Industry Leaders Association, and the Retail Council of Canada.[35]

ISSUES FOR CONGRESS

Congressional options relating to the Rana Plaza collapse may cover a range of issues, including allowing the situation to resolve itself. Broadly speaking, Congress may wish to conduct oversight and examine a comprehensive effort by the international community to support change in Bangladesh.

Key questions for Congress include the following:

- Is the ILO/World Bank Better Work program an effective approach, and has it been implemented successfully in other countries? Can it be expedited for Bangladesh?
- Should GSP eligibility for Bangladesh be reconsidered? Conversely, should tariff benefits for apparel be extended to Bangladesh to support it in improving the safety conditions of its workers?[36] Are there other steps the U.S. government should take?
- Have corporate codes of conduct been helpful?
- Will the Bangladesh Parliament approve the proposed changes that the ILO has recommended, and if so, will the ILO monitor their implementation?
- What are possible unintended consequences for Bangladeshi apparel workers if action leads to a decline in the apparel industry?

End Notes

[1] For background on Bangladesh, see CRS Report R41194, Bangladesh: Political and Strategic Developments and U.S. Interests, by Bruce Vaughn.

[2] According to press reports, European retailers were the primary purchasers. H&M is reportedly the largest producer of garments in Bangladesh. Source: "Global Retailers join Safety Plan for Bangladesh," The New York Times, May 14, 2013, p. A1.

[3] "17 Days in Darkness, a Cry of 'Save Me', and Joy," The New York Times, Saturday, May 11, 2012, p. A1

[4] "Bangladesh Finds Gross Negligence in Factory Fire," New York Times, Dec. 17, 2012.

[5] U.S. Department of State, Country Reports on Human Rights Practices, Bangladesh, p. 39.

[6] "Bangladesh Textile Factories Shut Amid Unrest," BBC News, May 13, 2013.

[7] Disney has announced it will leave Bangladesh and relocate elsewhere. Source: "Bangladesh Fears an Exodus of Apparel Firms," The New York Times, May 2, 2013.

[8] See CRS Report R41194, Bangladesh: Political and Strategic Developments and U.S. Interests, by Bruce Vaughn.

[9] "Western Firms Feel Pressure as Toll Rises in Bangladesh," The New York Times, April 25, 2013.

[10] Bangladesh approved the following conventions relating to ILO core labor principles: freedom of association and right to organize: C87, 1972; C98, 1972; elimination of forced labor: C29, 1972; C105, 1972; abolition of child labor: C138 (not approved by the Bangladeshi government); C182, 2001; and elimination of employment and occupational discrimination: C100, 1998; C111, 1972.

[11] While the ILO does not hold a core labor principle on occupational safety and health, this principle is included in a larger list of nearly 200 ILO principles. The ILO also publishes background materials on fire risk management. See, for example, the ILO booklet on Fire Risk Management, and its "Action Checklist Fire Safety," available on the ILO website at ilo.org.

[12] Issues in this section are also addressed in U.S. free trade agreements, which are not addressed in this report because the United States does not have a free trade agreement with Bangladesh.

[13] For more information on the GSP program, see CRS Report RL33663, Generalized System of Preferences: Background and Renewal Debate, by Vivian C. Jones.

[14] Among other criteria, there is a waiver of presidential authority based on U.S. national economic interest.

[15] These include the employment/use of children for purposes relating to armed conflict, drug trafficking, sex trafficking, or pornography.

[16] Office of the U.S. Trade Representative (USTR) Requests Comments on Bangladesh GSP Labor Eligibility Review, World Trade Online, January 10, 2013. See also, Pre-Hearing Brief Concerning the Petition to Remove Bangladesh From the List of Eligible Beneficiary Developing Countries Pursuant to Section 19 U.S.C. 2462(d) of the Generalized System of Preferences (GSP), filed by the AFL-CIO March, 2013.

[17] Source of data: U.S. International Trade Commission (USITC) Dataweb. While one option might involve oversight on possible suspension of GSP status for Bangladesh, as the USTR is considering, some experts have suggested considering, as an alternative, extending tariff-free treatment for apparel, to Bangladesh, perhaps in conjunction with a proposed ILO Better Work Bangladesh program under consideration. See "How to Avoid Another Bangladesh Factory Disaster," by Kimberly Elliot, Center for Global Development, May 7, 2013.

[18] For an overview of corporate codes of conduct, see CRS Report RS20803, Codes of Conduct for Multinational Corporations: An Overview, by James K. Jackson.

[19] Disney has announced it will leave Bangladesh and relocate elsewhere. Source: "Bangladesh Fears an Exodus of Apparel Firms," The New York Times, May 2, 2013.

[20] House Ways and Means Committee, "Levin, Miller Urge Action on Bangladeshi Worker Rights, Working Conditions", May 1, 2013. The Worker Rights Consortium, a labor rights monitoring group, estimates that it would cost $600,000, on average, to elevate each of Bangladesh's nearly 5,000 factories to western safety standards, for a total of $3 billion. This $3 billion can be compared against a Bangladesh world export market of about $20 billion in 2011. Source: "How to Fix Bangladesh's Factories," Bloomberg Business week, May 12, 2013.

[21] The other signatories of the letter are Senators Harkin, Durbin, Levin, Leahy, Murray, and Rockefeller. The letters were sent to the following retailers: the Cato Corporation, Walmart, Sears, Kohl's Target, Macy's JCPenney, Gap, Mango, George Westin Limited, VF Corporation, The Children's Place Stores, and Corte Ingles. Source: "Reid, Brown, Six Other Senators Call on Retailers to Sign Accord Guaranteeing Worker Safety in Bangladesh," World Trade Online, May 16, 2013.

[22] "House Dems, Faith Groups join Chorus Calling For U.S. Retailers to Sign Bangladesh Worker Safety Accord: Letter from 10 House Democrats," World Trade Online, May 16, 2013. Additional signatories are Representatives Sander Levin, George Miller, Lewis, Schakowsky, DeLauro, Becerra, Crowley, and Michaud. The U.S. retailers are The Gap, JC

Penney, The Children's Place, Walmart, Target, Kohl's, VF Corporation, Macy's, and Sears/Kmart.

[23] U.S. Department of State, "State Department Call With U.S. Buyers in Bangladesh Ready-Made Garment Sector," May 8, 2013; and "State Department Bureau of International Information Programs, Bangladesh, Private Partners Work to Improve Worker Safety," May 9, 2013.

[24] "Labor Dept. Offers $2.5 Million in Grants to Improve Will Fund Projects to Improve Bangladeshi Factory Conditions," by Niraj Chokshim National Journal, Government Executive, June 13, 2013.

[25] ILO, "Conclusions of the I LO's High Level Mission to Bangladesh." May 4, 2013. This program is jointly sponsored by the ILO and the International Finance Committee (IFC), a member of the World Bank Group.

[26] ILO, "Better Work Bangladesh – Design Phase," January 5, 2012; and "Bangladesh is Barred from Textile Safety Group," The Washington Post, May 18, 2013.

[27] "Global Retailers Join Safety Plan for Bangladesh; Will Pay for Changes," The New York Times, May 14, 2012, p. A1.

[28] "Bangladesh to Reform Labour Laws After Tragedy", Financial Times, May 6, 2013, p. 4; "Bangladesh Factory Toll Passes 800—Government Shuts 18 Sites for Safety Improvements, but No Big Outflow of U.S. Companies Seen," Wall Street Journal, May 9, 2013; and "Global Retailers Join Safety Plan for Bangladesh; Will Pay for Changes," The New York Times, May 14, 2013.

[29] "After Disaster, PR Tactics Vary; Some Clothing Firms Quickly Concede Links to Unsafe Bangladesh Factory. Others Hedge," Los Angeles Times, May 9, 2013.

[30] "Bangladesh Fears an Exodus of Apparel Firms," The New York Times, May 2, 2013.

[31] "Some Retailers Rethink Their Role in Bangladesh," The New York Times, May 1, 2013.

[32] "Global Retailers Join Safety Plan for Bangladesh," The New York Times, May14, 2013, p. A1. Bangladesh Factory Safety Accord: At Least 14 Major North American Retailers Decline to Sign, The Huffington Post, May 17, 2013. See also "H&M, Primark, Others Sign Legally Binding Agreement on Building, Fire Safety In Bangladesh: Reactions: Walmart; The Gap," Inside U.S. Trade, May 14, 2013.

[33] "Retailers Key to Bangladesh Worker Safety, Investors Tell Walmart, Gap," AFL-CIO, May 17, 2013.

[34] "Global Retailers Join Safety Plan for Bangladesh," The New York Times, May14, 2013, p. A1. Bangladesh Factory Safety Accord: At Least 14 Major North American Retailers Decline to Sign, The Huffington Post, May 17, 2013. See also "H&M, Primark, Others Sign Legally Binding Agreement on Building, Fire Safety In Bangladesh: Reactions: Walmart; The Gap," Inside U.S. Trade, May 14, 2013.

[35] "Miller Says Bangladesh Must Improve Labor Terms of Face GSP Loss," Inside U.S. Trade's World Trade Online, June 6, 2013.

[36] While one option might involve possible suspension of GSP status for Bangladesh, as the USTR is considering, some experts have also suggested as an alternative extending tariff-free treatment for apparel to Bangladesh, perhaps in conjunction with a proposed ILO Better Work Bangladesh program under consideration. See "How to Avoid Another Bangladesh Factory Disaster," by Kimberly Elliot, Center for Global Development, May 7, 2013.

In: Bangladesh
Editor: Gregory P. Davis

ISBN: 978-1-63117-003-4

Chapter 3

BANGLADESH 2012 HUMAN RIGHTS REPORT[*]

U.S. Department of State

EXECUTIVE SUMMARY

Bangladesh is a parliamentary democracy. Prime Minister Sheikh Hasina led the Awami League (AL) to victory in the 2008 parliamentary elections, which international and domestic observers considered free and fair, although with isolated irregularities and sporadic violence. In most instances security forces reported to civil authorities.

The most significant human rights problems were enforced disappearances, discrimination against marginalized groups, and poor working conditions and labor rights. Suspected extrajudicial killings, disappearances, and kidnappings continued, with human rights groups alleging the involvement of the country's security services. Marginalized groups, particularly Rohingya refugees, indigenous people, and women, suffered from unequal treatment and in some instances violence. Workers continued to face difficulties in forming unions and suffered from poor safety conditions in factories, highlighted by a factory fire on November 24.

[*] This is an edited, reformatted and augmented version of the U.S. Department of State; Bureau of Democracy, Human Rights and Labor, dated April 2013.

Other human rights problems included arbitrary arrests, detentions, and custodial deaths. Weak judicial capacity and resultant lengthy pretrial detentions continued to be problems. Authorities infringed on citizens' privacy rights. There were instances in which the government limited freedom of speech and assembly. Some journalists practiced self-censorship. Politically motivated violence and pervasive official corruption remained problems. Some nongovernmental organizations (NGOs) faced legal and informal restrictions on their activities. Many children were compelled to work, due either to economic necessity or in some instances trafficking. Discrimination against persons with disabilities was a problem, especially for children seeking admittance to public school. Instances of societal violence against religious and ethnic minorities persisted, although many government and civil society leaders claimed these acts had political or economic motivations and should not be attributed only to religious beliefs or affiliations. Child marriage of girls was a problem. Discrimination against persons based on their sexual orientation continued. Workers faced obstacles to engaging in collective bargaining. Child labor, particularly in the informal sector, remained a problem.

Official corruption and related impunity remained problems. Weak regard for the rule of law not only enabled individuals, including government officials, to commit human rights violations with impunity but also prevented citizens from claiming their rights. As in the previous year, the government did not take comprehensive measures to investigate and prosecute cases of security force killings.

Section 1. Respect for the Integrity of the Person, Including Freedom from

a. Arbitrary or Unlawful Deprivation of Life

The constitution provides for right to life and personal liberty; however, there were reports that the government or its agents committed arbitrary or unlawful killings.

The government neither released statistics on total killings by all security personnel nor took comprehensive measures to investigate cases, despite statements by high- ranking officials that the government would show "zero tolerance" and fully investigate all extrajudicial killings by security forces.

According to the media and local human rights organizations, no case resulted in criminal punishment and, in the few instances in which the government brought charges, those found guilty generally received administrative punishment. Some members of the security forces acted with impunity. In 2011 the government formed an internal inquiries cell within the paramilitary Rapid Action Battalion (RAB) to investigate cases of human rights abuses, but during the year the government did not disclose information on any prosecutions for suspected killings by RAB officers.

According to media reports, local and international human rights organizations, and the government, 70 persons were killed extrajudicially. These organizations believed RAB was responsible for 40 of the extrajudicial deaths, while combined security units consisting of RAB members killed six additional persons during the year. The deaths occurred during raids, arrests, and other law-enforcement operations. The government often described these deaths as "crossfire killings," "gunfights," or "encounter killings," terms used to characterize exchanges of gunfire between RAB or police units and criminal gangs. According to the NGO Odhikar, non-RAB law enforcement officials were responsible for 24 extrajudicial killings, down from 33 incidents in 2011.

A Ministry of Home Affairs (MHA) report on the April killing of Aminul Islam, a labor union organizer, suggested that collusion between the National Security Intelligence (NSI) and garment manufacturers was one of several reasons for his death (see section 7.a.).

Odhikar reported that, on June 10, Mohammad Abdul Wahab was shot and killed by police fire during a public protest at the Betai Chondipur police camp. While authorities formed a special investigation team to assess whether the police shooting was justified, police did not release the results of the investigation. According to the human rights organization Ain O-Shalish Kendra (ASK), there were 101 deaths in custody during the year, including 34 deaths in prison. Some of the deaths were allegedly the result of torture (see section 1.c.).

According to Odhikar, 169 persons were killed and 17,161 injured in political violence. In the AL, there were 382 incidents of internal violence; 146 such incidents were also recorded in the Bangladesh Nationalist Party (BNP) during this period. There were 37 persons and 4,330 injured in internal conflicts in the AL, while six were killed and 1,619 injured in the BNP's internal conflicts. These incidents were often linked to criminal activities rather than political motives. Incidents of nonlethal, politically motivated violence also occurred (see section 1.c.).

In one example of political violence related to a general strike, on December 9, members of the student wing of the ruling party, the Chattro League, beat and killed a passerby, 24-year-old Biswajit Das, because they thought he belonged to the opposition party. The killing gained national press coverage due to the brutal nature of the beating and the fact that multiple photo and television journalists captured the incident. Police arrested 10 men involved in the killing.

b. Disappearance

Disappearances and kidnappings, some by security services such as RAB and the Criminal Investigative Division, continued during the year. According to Odhikar, there were 24 disappearances with alleged ties to security personnel compared with 30 in 2011. Odhikar claimed that RAB was involved in 10 of these disappearances. The ASK estimated there were 56 enforced disappearances.

On June 13, Mohammad Nazrul Islam was arrested by members of RAB-12 while working on his farm and subsequently disappeared from Khamarkhand, Sirajgang. According to Odhikar's fact-finding report, two eyewitnesses asked the officers why they were taking Nazrul, and they responded by identifying themselves as RAB-12 and showing identity cards. No one has seen Nazrul since he was forcefully taken to the local RAB office. Eyewitnesses near the RAB office confirmed that officers took Nazrul there on the evening of June 13. When Nazrul's wife and son-in-law went to the office on June 14, RAB officials stated that Nazrul was not there; they could not locate him at any other law enforcement office. On June 16, Nazrul's wife filed an abduction report at the Kamarkhand police station. At year's end the investigation into Nazrul's whereabouts continued but remained inconclusive.

The MHA published two reports on high-profile disappearances. In its report on Tushar Islam Titu, leader of the Jubo League (the youth league of the AL), who disappeared in 2008, the committee found RAB to be responsible. The MHA named five perpetrators, each of whom denied involvement: Deputy Assistant Director of RAB-3 Mohammad Hanif, Assistant Sub-Inspector Firoze Ahmed, Corporal Amin Ullah Apu, Assistant Sub-Inspector Humayun Farid, and Deputy Assistant Director of RAB-2 Mokhlesur Rahman. RAB Public Relations Director Commander M. Sohail claimed the MHA report was erroneous.

There was no information on the 2011 disappearances of Iman Mohammad Rafiqul Islam or students Al-Mukaddas and Mohammad Waliulla.

c. Torture and Other Cruel, Inhuman, or Degrading Treatment or Punishment

Although the constitution and law prohibit torture and other cruel, inhuman, or degrading treatment or punishment, security forces, including RAB and police, reportedly employed torture and physical and psychological abuse during arrests and interrogations. Security forces used threats, beatings, and electric shock. According to Odhikar, security forces tortured at least 72 persons, killing seven. The government rarely charged, convicted, or punished those responsible.

The law contains provisions allowing a magistrate to place a suspect in interrogative custody, known as remand, during which the suspect can be questioned without a lawyer present. The government made efforts to limit remand because of instances of abuse occurring during remand.

For example, while held in remand on April 22, S.M. Mahmudul Huq Tito, a leader of the student wing of the BNP, was suspended by his arms from hooks in the ceiling by the officer in charge of the Khulna police, S.M. Kamruzzaman. According to several major news reports, the government reassigned Kamruzzaman from the Khulna police station through a bureaucratic procedure called "closing" but did not charge him in court.

According to Odhikar, there were 13 recorded incidents of rape and sexual abuse by members of law enforcement agencies. Five victims were under the age of 17. For example, on August 21, Odhikar reported that police constable Rashel Rana of the Atoltila police camp raped an 11-year-old girl in the Dighinala subdistrict of Khagrachori. The girl's family filed a case against Rana. A court jailed Rana, and the case remained under investigation.

Prison and Detention Center Conditions

Prison system conditions remained harsh and at times life threatening due to overcrowding, inadequate facilities, and lack of proper sanitation. Human rights observers stated that these conditions contributed to custodial deaths.

According to Odhikar, 58 persons died in prison compared with 105 prison deaths in 2011. In a July 4 report on the trials of Bangladesh Rifles mutineers, Human Rights Watch (HRW) documented 47 cases of custodial death between 2009 and 2012, some due to torture or mistreatment.

Physical Conditions: Media and human rights observers reported the prison population to be approximately 68,700 in a system designed to hold 33,570. Approximately one-third of the prison population had been convicted, with the rest awaiting trial or detained for investigation. Pretrial detainees often were incarcerated with convicted prisoners.

Due to overcrowding, prisoners slept in shifts and did not have adequate toilet facilities. All prisoners have the right to medical care and water. Human rights organizations and the media stated that some prisoners did not enjoy these rights. Water available in prisons was comparable with water available in the rest of the country, which was often not potable.

Conditions in prisons and often within the same prison complex varied widely because some prisoners were lodged in areas subject to high temperatures, poor ventilation, and overcrowding while others were placed in "divisional" custody, which featured better conditions, including increased family visitation and access to household staff.

The law requires that juveniles be held separately from adults, but in practice many juveniles were incarcerated with adults. Children were sometimes imprisoned (occasionally with their mothers) despite laws and court decisions prohibiting the imprisonment of minors.

Authorities routinely housed female prisoners separately from men. Although the law prohibits women in "safe custody" (usually victims of rape, trafficking, and domestic violence) from being housed with criminals, officials did not always provide separate facilities. According to Odhikar, 2,435 women were incarcerated in prisons, including 1,787 women awaiting trial and 648 who were convicted prisoners.

Administration: Prison recordkeeping was adequate. Authorities did not use alternatives to sentencing for nonviolent offenders, and prison ombudsmen were not available to prisoners. Authorities permitted religious observance for prisoners. They allowed prisoners to submit uncensored complaints and occasionally investigated such complaints.

Monitoring: The government generally did not permit prison visits by independent human rights monitors, including Odhikar and the International Committee of the Red Cross, but allowed the Bangladesh Red Crescent Society to visit foreign detainees. Government-appointed committees composed of prominent private citizens in each prison locality monitored prisons monthly but did not publicly release their findings. District judges occasionally visited prisons.

d. Arbitrary Arrest or Detention

The constitution prohibits arbitrary arrest and detention. The law permits authorities to arrest and detain persons suspected of criminal activity without an order from a magistrate or a warrant.

Legal experts and human rights activists criticized the use of mobile courts headed by magistrates during nationwide strikes called by the opposition party. Mobile courts immediately prosecuted persons who supported the strikes and rendered verdicts that often included prison terms.

Fearing widespread violence, law enforcement agencies arrested 3,215 persons in connection with a large rally organized by the opposition parties on March 12. Media and human rights observers noted that police arrested some day laborers, rickshaw pullers, hawkers, street vendors, and transport workers who were not involved in the rally along with political activists.

Role of the Police and Security Apparatus

Police, organized nationally under the MHA, have a mandate to maintain internal security and law and order. The army, organized under the Prime Minister's Office, is responsible for external security but also has some domestic security responsibilities, such as in the Chittagong Hills Tracts (CHT).

Civilian authorities maintained effective control over the armed forces, and the government has mechanisms to investigate and punish abuse and corruption. However, these mechanisms were not regularly employed in practice. The government took steps to improve police professionalism, discipline, training, and responsiveness, and to reduce corruption. For example, RAB established an internal affairs unit consisting of 20 officers, which investigated 12 cases and took action, including arrest, against three of the accused officers. Police incorporated instruction on the use of force into their basic training as part of a campaign to implement community-based policing.

Despite such efforts, security forces, including RAB, continued sometimes to commit abuses with impunity. Plaintiffs sometimes were reluctant to accuse police in criminal cases due to lengthy trial procedures and fears of retribution. Reluctance to bring charges against police also perpetuated a climate of impunity.

Security forces sometimes failed to prevent societal violence (see section 2.d.).

Arrest Procedures and Treatment While in Detention

The law provides for arrest on suspicion of criminal activity without an order from a magistrate or a warrant, and the government regularly used such provisions. The government or a district magistrate may order a person detained for 30 days to prevent the commission of an act that could threaten national security; however, authorities sometimes held detainees for longer periods. A magistrate must inform a detainee of the grounds for detention within 15 days, and an advisory board is required to examine the detainee's case after four months. Detainees have the right to appeal.

There is a functioning bail system in the regular courts. Criminal detainees charged with crimes were granted access to attorneys. The government sometimes provided detainees with state-funded defense attorneys. The few legal aid programs for detainees that existed were underfunded. Authorities generally permitted defense lawyers to meet with their clients after formal charges were filed in the courts, which in some cases occurred several weeks or months after the initial arrest.

Arbitrary Arrest: Arbitrary arrests occurred, usually in conjunction with political demonstrations, and the government held persons in detention without specific charges, sometimes in an attempt to collect information about other suspects. Following national political demonstrations on March 12, police arrested more than 3,000 suspected protestors. Odhikar estimated that the total number of arrests for the year was 8,675.

Pretrial Detention: Arbitrary and lengthy pretrial detention continued to be a problem due to bureaucratic inefficiencies, limited resources, lax enforcement of pretrial rules, and corruption. An estimated two million civil and criminal cases were pending. According to a 2008 estimate from the International Center for Prison Studies, nearly 70 percent of prison inmates, or 56,000 prisoners, were in pretrial detention. In some cases the length of pretrial detention equaled or exceeded the sentence for the alleged crime.

The International Crimes Tribunal continued to hold defendants for long periods of time without charging them. In one case, Mir Quasem Ali, who was arrested on June 17, was still under detention without charge at the end of the year. The enabling statute for the tribunal allows it to hold defendants without trial and to interrogate suspects without the presence of attorneys, and it routinely did so.

e. Denial of Fair Public Trial

The law provides for an independent judiciary, but a longstanding temporary provision of the constitution undermined full judicial independence in practice. According to the provision, the executive branch is in charge of the lower courts, judicial appointments, and compensation for judicial officials.

HRW reported that law enforcement and government officials intimidated defense counsel for leaders of the Islamic political party Jamaat-e-Islami who were accused of war crimes.

Corruption and a substantial backlog of cases hindered the court system, and extended continuances effectively prevented many defendants from obtaining fair trials due to witness tampering, victim intimidation, and missing evidence. Human rights observers stated that magistrates, attorneys, and court officials demanded bribes from defendants in many cases filed during the year.

Trial Procedures

The law provides for the right to a fair trial, but the judiciary could not always protect this right due to corruption and weak human and institutional capacities. Prosecutors and judges were underpaid, and their low monthly retainer of 3,000 taka (approximately $37) plus 200 taka (approximately $2.50) per hour in court meant some were willing to accept bribes to influence the outcome of a case. Defendants are presumed innocent and have the right to appeal and to see the government's evidence. Defendants have the right to be informed promptly and in detail of the charges against them. The law prevented undue delay of proceedings for certain offenses, such as murder, sexual assault, and robbery. Judges rather than juries decide cases, and trials are public. Indigent defendants have the right to a public defender. Defendants also have adequate time to prepare a defense; adjournments are one factor that contributed to the backlog of cases. Accused persons have the right to be represented by counsel, review accusatory material, call or question witnesses, and appeal verdicts, and the government sometimes respected these rights.

The courts used mass trials for Bangladesh Rifles mutineers, with up to 800 of the accused standing trial at the same time in military proceedings. HRW called for mass trial proceedings to cease and for each individual to be charged and tried for his own alleged crime. Most mutiny trials were completed by October 21, with 5,926 mutineers serving prison sentences ranging from four months to seven years. Cases for serious crimes associated with the mutiny, including murder, arson, and looting, continued in civilian courts at year's end.

Political Prisoners and Detainees

While political affiliation was sometimes a factor in the arrest and prosecution of members of the opposition parties, no persons were prosecuted solely for political reasons.

Civil Judicial Procedures and Remedies

Individuals and organizations may seek administrative and judicial remedies for human rights violations; however, the civil court system was slow and cumbersome, deterring many from filing complaints. The government did not interfere with civil judicial procedures. Corruption and outside influence were problems in the civil judicial system. Alternative dispute resolution for civil cases allows citizens to present their cases for mediation. According to government sources, the wider use of mediation in civil cases accelerated the administration of justice, but there was no assessment of its fairness or impartiality.

Property Restitution

The government did not take action to compensate individuals, primarily Hindus, who lost their land under the 1974 Vested Property Act, despite the change to the law in 2001 requiring the return of the land (see section 2.d.).

f. Arbitrary Interference with Privacy, Family, Home, or Correspondence

The law does not prohibit arbitrary interference with private correspondence; rather, intelligence and law enforcement agencies may monitor private communications with the permission of the chief executive of the MHA. Police rarely obtained warrants as required, and authorities did not punish officers who violated these procedures. Human rights organizations alleged that the special branch of police, the NSI, and the Directorate General Forces Intelligence employed informers to conduct surveillance and report on citizens perceived to be critical of the government. The government also routinely conducted surveillance on opposition politicians. Human rights organizations and news outlets reported that police sometimes entered private homes without obtaining proper authorization.

SECTION 2. RESPECT FOR CIVIL LIBERTIES, INCLUDING

a. Freedom of Speech and Press

The constitution provided for these rights, but the government sometimes failed to respect freedom of speech and press. There were some limitations on freedom of speech and perceived misrepresentation or defamation of Islam. Some journalists self-censored their criticisms of the government due to harassment.

Freedom of Speech: The constitution equates criticism of the constitution with sedition. Punishment for sedition ranges from three years' to life imprisonment. During the year the courts did not sentence anyone under these laws. The law limits hate speech but does not define clearly what constitutes hate speech, leaving the government with broad powers of interpretation. The government can restrict speech deemed to be against the security of the state; against friendly relations with foreign states; against public order, decency, or morality; or that constitutes contempt of court, defamation, or incitement to an offense.

For example, university student Sohel Molla Raj (alias Sohel Rana) implied on his personal Facebook account that the prime minister was connected with Ilias Ali's disappearance (see section 1.b.). A university official filed a complaint with the Trishal police station, which filed a sedition charge against Sohel Rana with the MHA. The deputy commissioner of Mymensingh seconded the request to the MHA. On May 18, police arrested Sohel, whose his first court hearing was on July 9. Sohel remained detained in the Mymensingh jail.

Freedom of Press: The independent media were active and expressed a wide variety of views; however, media critical of the government sometimes experienced negative government pressure.

The government owned one radio station and one television station. The law mandates that the public television station, BTV, remain the country's only terrestrial (nonsatellite) broadcast channel. An estimated 60 percent of the population did not have access to private satellite channels, and surveys indicated that almost 80 percent of citizens received their information from television. BTV broadcast parliamentary sessions and government programming but rarely broadcast opposition views. Cable operators generally functioned without government interference. The government required all private stations to broadcast, without charge, selected government news programs and speeches by the prime minister.

Fiction writer Humayun Ahmed's recent novel *Dewal* discussed the killing of the country's first president, Sheikh Mujibur Rahman. On May 15, the High Court pronounced the novel "wrong and objectionable" and requested the government to order Ahmed to correct the "misinformation" in his book.

Police in Bogra continued to provide security for correspondent Hasibur Rahman Bilu of the newspaper *Daily Star* in compliance with a November 2011 High Court order. The order followed attacks and death threats in response to reports published in the *Daily Star* on alleged corruption by the ruling AL party leader in collusion with the then deputy commissioner.

Violence and Harassment: Journalists were subjected to physical attack, harassment, and intimidation from both state and nonstate actors. According to Odhikar and media watchdog groups, during the year four journalists were killed, 118 injured, 50 threatened, six attacked, and 43 assaulted.

On February 11, unknown assailants killed Sagar Sarwar, news editor of the private channel Maasranga TV, and his wife, Meherun Runi, a reporter for the private channel ATN Bangla. The Bangladesh Federal Union of Journalists protested the killings. After some media reports speculated on the killer's identity, on February 28, the Supreme Court ordered the press to refrain from publishing speculative news about the case. On October 10, police released the names of eight suspects, but family and colleagues of the deceased dismissed the findings. No one was arrested for the killings.

Privately owned Ekushey Television (ETV) faced harassment from the National Board of Revenue (NBR) and the Bangladesh Telecommunication Regulatory Commission (BTRC) following its failure to heed alleged demands by unnamed government officials to cancel two programs that discussed contemporary political issues. On January 12, the ETV Chairman, Abdus Salam, received a backdated letter from the NBR asking him to pay 128 million taka ($1.58 million) in past-due income taxes and fines. In July the NBR charged Salam with tax evasion. Salam claimed ETV did not owe any outstanding taxes. The case continued at year's end, and Salam's petition to have the case dismissed was pending.

Censorship or Content Restrictions: The government indirectly censored the media through threats and harassment. According to journalists, on multiple occasions government officials asked privately owned television channels not to broadcast the opposition's activities and statements. For example, ETV, Bangla Vision, and Islamic TV defied unofficial requests not to broadcast a live opposition alliance rally on March 12. Government intelligence officials allegedly forced cable operators to suspend the transmission of the three channels until after the rally ended. According to some journalists and human rights NGOs, journalists engaged in self-censorship due to fear of government retribution. Although public criticism of the government was common and vocal, the media--particularly print media--depended on government advertisements for a significant percentage of their revenue. As a result the media had an incentive for self-censorship.

This government, like its predecessors, issued new broadcast licenses to political supporters and denied them to political opponents.

The government did not subject foreign publications and films to stringent review and censorship. A government-managed film censor board reviewed local and foreign films and had the authority to censor or ban films on the grounds of state security, law and order, religious sentiment, obscenity, foreign relations, defamation, or plagiarism, but was less strict than in the past. In practice video rental libraries and DVD shops stocked a wide variety of films, and government efforts to enforce censorship on rentals were sporadic and ineffective.

The government at times censored immodest or obscene photographs or objectionable comments regarding national leaders.

There were no significant local government initiatives to foster media independence.

Internet Freedom

Individuals and groups could generally engage in the expression of views via the Internet. Access to the Internet was not widespread; the Internet had only a 3.5 percent penetration rate according to the International Telecommunication Union. The government blocked some Facebook pages, including pages depicting the Prophet Muhammad and pages critical of both the prime minister and opposition leader. On September 17, the Telecommunication and Radio Commission blocked YouTube. The BTRC previously asked YouTube's parent company, Google, to remove the video *The Innocence of Muslims* from YouTube and blocked access when Google did not comply. YouTube remained blocked at the year's end.

Academic Freedom and Cultural Events

The government had few restrictions on academic freedom or cultural events. Media groups reported that authorities discouraged research on sensitive religious and political topics that might fuel possible religious or communal tensions. In addition, some Dhaka University teachers, many with overt BNP affiliations, were dismissed or put on extended leave after the AL-led government assumed office in 2009; it was unclear whether the concerned teachers were targeted because of their political affiliations.

The government exerted particularly strict control of information in textbooks related to the country's independence. On March 6, the High Court directed authorities at the Bangladesh Open University to file a criminal complaint against three Dhaka University professors and 10 others deemed liable for distorting the Liberation War history in two open university textbooks. On May 9, a Dhaka court issued an arrest warrant for Ershadul Bari, former vice chancellor of the Bangladesh Open University, in connection with a charge of distorting Liberation War history. On April 5, the metropolitan magistrate summoned three persons including Bari for the second time, since they did not appear following the court's initial summons. On December 31, the court charged Bari with absconding and ordered police to confiscate his movable property.

b. Freedom of Peaceful Assembly and Association

The constitution provides for freedom of assembly and association, and the government generally respected these rights in practice; however, there were instances of governmental action to limit freedom of assembly during periods of political protest and unrest.

Freedom of Assembly

The government permitted rallies, and they occurred with great regularity. On occasion, citing fear of violence, the government prevented political groups from holding meetings and demonstrations. The law authorizes the government to ban assemblies of more than four persons; according to Odhikar, authorities used this provision at least 105 times during the year. Occasionally police or ruling party activists used force to disperse demonstrations.

In January the BNP called for a rally on March 12 in Dhaka to support the restoration of a caretaker government system to conduct elections. In February the AL announced it would also hold a rally in Dhaka on the same date. Citing concerns for public safety, the Dhaka Metropolitan Police banned human chains, protests, rallies, sit-ins, meetings, and processions for March

12. In addition, law enforcement authorities acted to prevent Dhaka-bound public transit and restricted traffic inside the city on March 11. Police arrested over 400 persons prior to March 12. Police ultimately allowed the opposition rally to proceed.

Various groups in the country planned protests against the video *The Innocence of Muslims*. In Dhaka these groups gathered outside the city's main mosque, Baitul Mukarram, following Friday afternoon prayers on September 14 and 21. Police allowed protesters to proceed as long as they were peaceful and did not march towards diplomatic missions. However, on September 21, the government banned public gatherings ahead of a long-planned rally of 12 Islamic parties set for September 22. The parties had intended to demand that the country's constitution establish Islam as the state religion and to condemn the video. Members of the parties defied the ban and attempted to protest, resulting in some arrests.

Jamaat-e-Islami reported that the government severely hampered its ability to secure permits for rallies or processions throughout the year. Government officials also prohibited Jamaat-e-Islami leaders from meeting at the party's headquarters.

Freedom of Association

The law provides for the right of citizens to form associations, subject to "reasonable restrictions" in the interest of morality or public order, and the government generally respected this right. Individuals were free to join private groups. Trade unions were able to conduct their normal activities such as collective bargaining, but government action made it nearly impossible to form new trade unions in many sectors, for example, in the ready-made garment and shrimp industries. The government also denied or delayed the registration of NGOs working in certain sensitive areas such as human rights, labor rights, or humanitarian assistance for Rohingya refugees. The government's NGO affairs bureau also withheld approval of foreign funding for such projects (see section 2.d.). There were reports of increasing scrutiny of and restrictions on activities of NGOs by the NGO affairs bureau.

c. Freedom of Religion

See the Department of State's *International Religious Freedom Report* at www.state.gov/j/drl/irf/rpt/.

d. Freedom of Movement, Internally Displaced Persons, Protection of Refugees, and Stateless Persons

The law provides for freedom of movement within the country, foreign travel, emigration, and repatriation, and the government generally respected these rights in practice, except in two sensitive areas, the CHT and Cox's Bazar.

The government did not fully cooperate with the Office of the UN High Commissioner for Refugees (UNHCR) and other humanitarian organizations in providing protection and assistance to refugees, asylum seekers, stateless persons, and other persons of concern.

Foreign Travel: Passport holders do not require exit permits or visas to leave the country. There were no special controls on women or minorities. Some senior opposition officials reported extensive delays in getting their passports renewed.

The international travel ban continued on war crimes suspects from the 1971 liberation war.

The country's passports are invalid for travel to Israel.

Internally Displaced Persons (IDPs)

Low-level armed conflict in the CHT between 1973 and 1997 rendered tens of thousands of indigenous persons internally displaced. During the conflict the government relocated landless Bengalis from the plains with the unstated objective of changing the demographic balance in the CHT towards a Bengali majority.

The International Displacement Monitoring Center (IDMC) also reported that members of religious minorities across the country were "forcibly displaced" as a result of discriminatory legislation. The IDMC reported nearly 750,000 Hindu families were dispossessed of agricultural land over the years. There was no systematic reporting on the treatment of these widely scattered IDPs. The government did not make progress in implementing laws to restore property (see section 1.e.).

IDPs in the CHT had limited physical security. Indigenous community leaders suggested that settlers' violations of indigenous persons' rights, sometimes with the involvement of security forces, were widespread.

IDPs in the CHT also lacked sufficient access to courts and legal aid. The CHT Commission, composed of experts from inside and outside the country who sought to promote respect for human rights, democracy, participatory development, and land rights in the CHT, found that a lack of information and lawyers to assist indigenous persons hindered IDPs' access to justice. The CHT Commission reported that settlers expropriated indigenous land using false titles, intimidation, force, fraud, and manipulation of government eminent-domain claims.

The number of IDPs in the CHT remained disputed. In 2000 a government task force estimated the number to be 500,000 but included nonindigenous persons in its estimate. During the same year, Amnesty International reported approximately 60,000 indigenous IDPs. These were the most recent estimates available. The prime minister pledged to resolve outstanding land disputes in the CHT to facilitate the return of IDPs and to close the remaining military camps. No land disputes were resolved during the year.

Protection of Refugees

The government and the UNHCR provided temporary protection and basic assistance to 30,000 Rohingya refugees from Burma living in two official camps (Kutapalong and Nayapara). The UNHCR estimated that an additional 220,000 undocumented Rohingya lived in the Cox's Bazar, Bandarban, and Chittagong districts, while the government estimated that 200,000 to 500,000 undocumented Rohingya resided during the year in various villages and towns outside the two official refugee camps. Most of these undocumented Rohingya lived among the local population in Teknaf and Ukhyia in Cox's Bazar district, including approximately 20,000 at an unofficial site adjacent to the official Kutupalong refugee camp and approximately 9,000 at the Leda site.

Access to Asylum: The country's laws do not provide for granting asylum or refugee status, and the government has not established a formal system for providing protection to refugees. The government did not issue a review of its refugee policy, which the Ministry of Foreign Affairs stated it would do after suspending all resettlement programs in 2010. The government provided some protection to Rohingya refugees from Burma already resident in the country, but it continued to deny asylum to Rohingya whom it categorized as illegal economic migrants. While the government cooperated with the UNHCR in providing temporary protection and basic assistance to officially registered refugees already resident in two official camps, it did not cooperate with the UNHCR to expand services to undocumented Rohingya, who were persons of concern to the UNHCR, or new arrivals fleeing the violence in bordering Rakhine State, Burma. During sectarian violence in Burma's northern Rakhine State in June and again in October, the government closed its borders and pushed asylum seekers fleeing attacks back into Burma.

Refoulement: Continued violence and human rights abuses against the Rohingya in Burma prevented the government from assisting the safe, voluntary return of refugees to their homes. The Ministry of Foreign Affairs and the Border Guard Bangladesh forcibly returned an estimated 6,163 Rohingya to Burma, where their lives or freedoms may have been threatened. According to the UNHCR, many individuals who were turned back likely were entitled to refugee status and protection. Despite these pushbacks, the border remained porous. The UNHCR, which maintained a field presence in both countries and monitored these trends, acknowledged considerable daily cross-border movement for trade, smuggling, and, after June, illegal migration.

Refugee Abuse: The UNHCR reported cases of refugee abuse, including rape, assault, domestic abuse, deprivation of food, arbitrary detention, and documentation problems.

Employment: The government did not allow Rohingya refugees living in the country on an extended basis to work locally. Refugees had limited freedom of movement beyond the camps and had to obtain permission for all movement outside the camps. Despite these constraints, some refugees worked illegally as manual laborers or rickshaw pullers in the informal economy. Undocumented Rohingya also worked illegally, mostly in day-labor jobs.

Access to Basic Services: Working with the UNHCR, the government continued to improve some aspects of the official refugee camps following findings in recent years that sanitation, nutrition, and shelter conditions had fallen below minimum international standards. Some basic standards remained unmet, and conditions in the camps continued to be overcrowded, with densities on par with the country's urban slums. On October 2, the UNHCR and the World Food Program released a nutrition survey report that stated the prevalence of malnourished (stunted) and underweight children in refugee camps remained higher than in the rest of the country and was near the emergency threshold levels set by the World Health Organization.

Public education is mandatory through the eighth grade throughout the country, but was offered only through fifth grade in the camps. Refugees were not allowed to attend school beyond the fifth grade outside the camps; however, small numbers of students studied with the assistance of private tutors and participated in countrywide school examinations through the high school level. By law unregistered refugees are not allowed to attend public schools, but many attended in practice.

Neither registered nor unregistered refugees were allowed access to public health care. However, the provision of basic health services by the UNHCR and NGOs meant that registered refugees often received better medical care than citizens in surrounding villages. Although humanitarian assistance provided by NGOs served registered Rohingya refugees, undocumented Rohingya, and the local Bangladeshi population, the government's restrictions on NGO activities outside the camps limited the unregistered population's access to basic medical care and other services.

International NGOs faced difficulties in providing basic services to undocumented Rohingya and to the surrounding impoverished host communities because the NGO affairs bureau refused to grant permission for them to operate. Extended delays by the government's NGO affairs bureau in granting approvals also made it difficult for international NGOs to operate in the country and to implement assistance programs. The NGO affairs bureau ordered three NGOs--Doctors without Borders (MSF), Action against Hunger (ACF), and Muslim Aid--that were providing basic assistance, such as water and sanitation, healthcare, and education, to unregistered Rohingya to cease their activities as of July 30. The NGOs reduced their operations to provide only life-saving services.

Registered refugees did not have the right to legal recourse through the country's formal legal system, although they were able to take legal complaints to a local camp official, who could mediate disputes. The members of the unregistered population had no legal protection and were sometimes arrested because the government viewed them as illegal economic migrants.

Durable Solutions: There were no Rohingya voluntarily repatriated to Burma or resettled in third countries. Although the situation remained protracted, the government did not facilitate local integration by conducting a census or considering any regularization of the Rohingya's status, such as naturalization.

Stateless Persons

The Rohingya in the country are legally stateless. This group of Rohingya cannot derive citizenship from birth in the country or from marriage with local citizens. The laws do not afford Rohingya any opportunity to gain nationality.

SECTION 3. RESPECT FOR POLITICAL RIGHTS: THE RIGHT OF CITIZENS TO CHANGE THEIR GOVERNMENT

The constitution provides citizens the right to change their government peacefully, and citizens exercised this right in practice through periodic, free, and fair elections based on universal suffrage.

On September 16, the Supreme Court released the text of its 2011 decision to abolish the practice of holding national elections during a temporary caretaker government. Subsequently, the main opposition party, the BNP, stated it would not participate in elections unless they were conducted under a nonpartisan administration. The opposition party has since boycotted subnational elections.

Elections and Political Participation

Recent Elections: Sheikh Hasina, the leader of the AL, became prime minister in 2009 following the most recent parliamentary elections in 2008, which international and local observers deemed free and fair. The 14-party AL alliance held 307 of the 350 seats in parliament. The opposition BNP and its allies held 41 seats. One seat belonged to an independent member and one seat remained vacant following the death of an AL member. Hasina's cabinet included representatives from the other parties in her coalition. BNP chairperson and former prime minister Khaleda Zia became leader of the opposition.

Political Parties: Opposition parties boycotted parliament throughout the year but returned on certain days to fulfill the requirements for them to retain their seats. In general they demanded fair treatment by the speaker and the ruling party legislators as preconditions for their return to the house. Opposition parties participated in all 48 standing parliamentary committees in the first session, despite their absence from parliament.

In some instances the government interfered with the right of opposition parties to organize public functions (see section 2.b.). It also manipulated the media to restrict broadcast of opposition political events (see section 2.a.).

Participation of Women and Minorities: There are no laws preventing women or minorities from voting or participating in political life. Women were eligible to contest any of the 300 seats in parliament, and an additional 50 seats were reserved for women. During the year there were 69 women in parliament, 19 of whom were directly elected and 50 who were chosen by political parties based on their proportional representation in parliament. Five women were full cabinet ministers. Three women served at the state ministerial level.

There is no provision to reserve parliamentary seats for minorities.

SECTION 4. CORRUPTION AND LACK OF TRANSPARENCY IN GOVERNMENT

The law provides criminal penalties for corruption by officials, but the government did not implement the law effectively. Human rights groups, the media, the Anticorruption Commission (ACC), and other institutions reported government corruption during the year. Officials frequently engaged in corrupt practices with impunity. The laws do not require elected or appointed officials to disclose their income and assets. The AL promised in its election manifesto that ministers and members of parliament would disclose their assets, but they did not.

The ACC is the government agency charged with fighting corruption. A 2010 World Bank report stated the government undermined the ACC's work and hampered the prosecution of corruption. The report stated that the government filed far fewer corruption cases than had the previous caretaker government and that a government commission recommended that the ACC drop thousands of corruption cases. Some in civil society stated that the government was not serious about fighting corruption and that the ACC was used for politically motivated prosecutions. Transparency International Bangladesh asserted that political interference in the ACC's operations had rendered it a "toothless tiger."

On June 29, the World Bank canceled its $1.2 billion Padma Bridge loan citing the government's failure to take specific measures that the bank required following the emergence in late 2011 of corruption allegations involving senior government officials. On September 20, the bank agreed to reengage in the project after the government implemented each of the measures, including removing certain individuals from public office and agreeing to the ACC's engagement with the bank's expert panel in pursuing the corruption allegations. The ACC determined there was sufficient evidence to investigate the role of seven senior officials; it subsequently filed formal charges against six and arrested two but at year's end had not opened an investigation of the former communications minister.

In another case, then railway minister Suranjit Sengupta was allegedly involved in bribe taking. Sengupta's assistant private secretary, Omar Faruq Talukder, and two other ministry officials were caught with 7.4 million taka (approximately $91,000) cash in their car. Sengupta's driver, Ali Azam, claimed the officials were taking the money to Sengupta's home as part of his share of a bribery deal involving appointments to the ministry. Sengupta maintained his innocence but submitted his resignation on April 16. The prime minister retained him as a minister without a portfolio. An inquiry by the Railway Ministry found Sengupta innocent, and the ACC refused to take action against him, stating that the driver later claimed ownership of the money. Azam continued to claim in private interviews that the money was intended for Sengupta. ACC chair Golam Rahman refused to take Azam's statement.

The government took steps to address widespread police corruption. The inspector general of police continued to implement a new strategy, partially funded by international donors, for training police, addressing corruption, and creating a more responsive police force. No assessment of the strategy's effect on corruption within the police force was available.

The judiciary was subject to political pressure from the government, and cases involving opposition leaders often proceeded in an irregular fashion. In several cases the appellate division overturned decisions granting bail to high-level corruption suspects who were leaders of opposition parties.

Corruption remained a serious problem within the judiciary and was a factor in lengthy delays of trials, which were subject to witness tampering and intimidation of victims. Several reports by human rights groups and corruption watchdog groups indicated growing public dissatisfaction with the perceived politicization of the judiciary.

The law provides for public access to government information, but in practice it was not fully effective. The Information Commission is responsible for implementing the law. The law lists a few exceptions (due to national security) and establishes nominal processing fees. The commission has the authority to issue summons if the relevant individuals do not comply with a request for information and to compel such individuals to give oral or written evidence under oath. Observers noted that the government filed few cases during the year due to limited understanding of the law and limited capacity to file and pursue requests for information. The commission conducted public outreach and training of public officials to encourage effective use of the law.

Section 5. Governmental Attitude Regarding International and Nongovernmental Investigation of Alleged Violations of Human Rights

A wide variety of domestic and international human rights groups generally operated independently and without government restriction, investigating and publishing their findings on human rights cases. Although human rights groups often were sharply critical of the government, they also practiced some self- censorship. Government officials were generally not cooperative and responsive to their views.

UN and Other International Bodies: The government required all NGOs, including religious organizations, to register with the Ministry of Social Welfare. Local and international NGOs working on selected, sensitive topics such as human rights, indigenous people, Rohingya refugees, or workers' rights faced both formal and informal governmental restrictions. HRW, Odhikar, MSF, ACF, Handicap International, and the Bangladesh Center for Workers' Solidarity (BCWS) reported numerous credible instances in which the government impeded their work, either by canceling projects or subjecting them to restrictive operating requirements that often resulted in a temporary or permanent cessation of their work. These groups also claimed that intelligence agencies monitored them. The government sometimes restricted international NGOs' ability to operate through delays in project registration and visa refusals.

The government countered NGO criticism through the media, sometimes with intimidating or threatening remarks. For example, on July 4, HRW reported that the mass trial of border guard mutineers was not free and fair and demanded the government disband the RAB. The government called the HRW report "false, baseless, and concocted" and stated that it was part of an "international conspiracy" supported by "local upstart organizations." Employees at Odhikar and ASK, the two local NGOs that supported HRW's research, received threats of arrest for sedition.

Government Human Rights Bodies: The National Human Rights Commission (NHRC) is a seven-member body, but five members are honorary. The NHRC has a small government support staff, and observers noted it was understaffed and underfunded. The NHRC's primary activity was educating the public about human rights, and the NHRC chairman made numerous media appearances. The NHRC received a "B" status from the International Council of Coordinating Committee of National Institutions for the Promotion and Protection of Human Rights (ICC), which found that the NHRC did not fully comply with international standards for such bodies. The ICC focused on the lack of transparency in selecting NHRC commissioners and NHRC's lack of hiring authority over its support staff.

SECTION 6. DISCRIMINATION, SOCIETAL ABUSES, AND TRAFFICKING IN PERSONS

Laws specifically prohibit certain forms of discrimination against women, provide special procedures for persons accused of violence against women and children, call for harsh penalties, provide compensation to victims, and require action against investigating officers for negligence or willful failure of duty; however, enforcement of these laws was weak. Women, children, minority groups, persons with disabilities, indigenous people, and sexual minorities often confronted social and economic disadvantages.

Women

Rape and Domestic Violence: The law prohibits rape and physical spousal abuse but makes no specific provision for spousal rape. According to Odhikar, during the year there were 805 reported incidents of rape against women and girls, including 299 women and 33 victims whose age could not be ascertained. According to human rights monitors, the actual number of rape cases was higher because many rape victims did not report the incidents due to social stigma or fear of further harassment. Prosecution of rapists was not consistent. Of the women, 31 were killed after being raped and 101 were victims of gang rape. ASK reported 1,008 rape cases, including 21 attempted rapes, filed with police during the year.

The law criminalizes domestic violence. Women's rights groups criticized the government for its inaction on domestic violence, and data were difficult to obtain. A 2000 study by the UN Population Fund indicated that at least 50 percent of women experienced domestic violence at least once in their lives. During the year the Bangladesh National Women Lawyers' Association (BNWLA) received more than 9,000 reports of violence against women and filed 731 cases related to violence against women. NGOs with little assistance from the government funded most efforts to combat domestic violence. NGOs such as the BNWLA operated shelters for destitute persons and distressed women and children. Courts sent most victims of domestic violence to shelter homes such as those run by BNWLA. In a few cases victims were sent to prison as a transitory destination for short periods. There were some support groups for victims of domestic violence.

Harmful Traditional Practices: Some of the reported violence against women was related to disputes over dowries. Odhikar reported 822 cases of dowry-related violence, the highest reported in four years. Of this number, 273 cases involved victims who were killed, 14 committed suicide, and 535 were mistreated.

On November 2, a pregnant housewife in Nageshwari, Kurigram, Khushina Khatun, was allegedly strangled to death by her husband, Mofizul Huq, over dowry demands. She died on the way to Rangpur Medical College Hospital. After her death her father filed a complaint against his daughter's in-laws at the Nageshwari police station. On December 18, the investigating officer informed Odhikar that, while the victim's father-in-law and mother-in-law were arrested, they did not arrest the prime suspect, Mofizul Huq.

On May 12, the Supreme Court's appellate division overruled a 2001 high court ruling prohibiting fatwas (religious edicts). However, in its ruling the court declared that fatwas could be used only to settle religious matters and could not be invoked to justify meting out punishment, nor could they supersede existing secular law. Islamic tradition dictates that only those religious scholars with expertise in Islamic law could declare a fatwa. Despite these restrictions village religious leaders sometimes made such declarations. The declarations resulted in extrajudicial punishments, often against women, for perceived moral transgressions.

Incidents of vigilantism against women, sometimes led by religious leaders enforcing fatwas, occurred. According to ASK, 48 incidents of vigilante violence against women occurred during the year and only 16 incidents resulted in police action. The incidents included whipping, beating, and other forms of physical violence.

Acid attacks, although less common than in the past, remained a serious problem. Assailants threw acid in the faces of victims--usually women--that left them disfigured and often blind. Acid attacks often related to a woman's refusal to accept a marriage proposal or to land disputes. Odhikar reported acid attacks on 58 women, 17 men, 20 girls, and 10 boys. The law seeks to control the availability of acid and reduce acid-related violence directed toward women, but lack of awareness of the law and poor enforcement limited its effect. The government made efforts to punish offenders and reduce the availability of acid to the general public. The Commerce Ministry restricted acid sales to buyers registered with relevant trade organizations; however, the restrictions were not universally enforced. The law provides for speedier prosecutions of acid-throwing cases in special tribunals and generally does not allow bail. According to the Acid Survivors Foundation, the special tribunals were not entirely effective, and prosecutors obtained a conviction in an estimated 8 to 10 percent of cases. Five persons were convicted in three cases during the year.

Sexual Harassment: Sexual harassment in public and private, including in educational institutions and workplaces, is a criminal offense; however, harassment remained a problem. In January 2011 the Supreme Court ordered police stations to report on sexual harassment monthly and to set up separate cells for men and women to prevent sexual harassment. Police did not fully comply with the court order. Odhikar reported 346 cases of harassment against women, although many incidents went unreported.

Reproductive Rights: Couples and individuals had the information to decide the number, spacing, and timing of children free from discrimination, coercion, or violence through access to a full range of contraceptive methods, including long- acting reversible contraception and permanent methods. While pharmacies carried a wide range of family planning options, low levels of income and education, and traditional family roles often served as barriers to access.

According to the *2010 Bangladesh Maternal Mortality and Health Care Survey*, the maternal mortality ratio declined by 40 percent over the preceding nine years, from 322 to 194 deaths per 100,000 live births. Approximately half of the maternal deaths were due to postpartum hemorrhage and eclampsia, with 7 percent attributed to obstructed or prolonged labor. According to the

2011 Bangladesh Demographic and Health Survey, 31.7 percent of births were delivered by a skilled birth attendant. Only 29 percent of the deliveries occurred at a health facility. Although 54.6 percent of women received at least one antenatal checkup from a medically trained provider, only 25.5 percent of women received the recommended four checkups following live births. Only 27 percent of the mothers received a postnatal check up from a trained provider within two days of delivery.

Discrimination: Women do not enjoy the same legal status and rights as men in family, property, and inheritance law. Under traditional Islamic inheritance laws, daughters inherit only half that of sons, and in the absence of sons they may inherit only what remains after settling all debts and other obligations. Under Hindu inheritance laws, a widow's rights to her deceased husband's property are limited to her lifetime and revert to the male heirs upon her death. The parliament passed the Hindu Marriage Registration Bill 2012, which allows for the optional registration of Hindu marriages. HRW reported that discriminatory personal laws affected Muslim, Hindu, and Christian women. It found women whose marriages ended often fell into poverty due to these legal provisions that make it difficult to obtain legal redress.

Employment opportunities increased for women, who constituted approximately 80 percent of garment factory workers. However, women were sometimes subjected to abuse in factories, including sexual harassment. There were some gender-based wage disparities in the overall economy, but wages of women and men were comparable in the garment sector. Women still faced difficulty in seeking access to credit and other economic opportunities, but the government's National Women's Development Policy included commitments to provide opportunities for women in employment and business.

Children

Despite strong legislation for children's rights, there is a general lack of enforcement due to limited resources and capacity to implement and monitor these laws. Governance remained weak with the responsibility for children held by one of the least-resourced ministries, the Ministry of Women and Children's Affairs. The government, with the assistance of local and foreign NGOs, worked to improve children's rights and welfare, enabling the country to make significant progress in improving children's health, nutrition, and education. Despite some progress, the 2011 Bangladesh Health Survey found that 41.3 percent of children remained chronically malnourished, as defined by moderate or severe levels of stunting (height for age). This was a decrease from 48.6 percent malnutrition in 2009.

Birth Registration: The law does not grant citizenship automatically by birth within the country. Individuals become citizens if their fathers or grandfathers were born in the territories that are now part of the country. If a person qualifies for citizenship through ancestry, the father or grandfather must have been a permanent resident of these territories in or after 1971. The government began a universal birth registration program in 2005, which increased the registration rate from 10 percent at the outset to 51 percent in 2010.

Education: Primary education was free and compulsory through the eighth grade, and the government offered subsidies to parents to keep girls in class through the 10th grade. Government incentives to families that sent children to school contributed significantly to the rise in primary school enrollments in recent years, but hidden school fees at the local level created barriers to access for the poorest families. Many families kept children out of school to become wage earners or to help with household chores, and primary school coverage was insufficient in remote and disaster-prone areas.

Child Abuse: All forms of child abuse, including sexual abuse, physically and humiliating punishment, child abandonment, abuse, kidnapping, and trafficking continued to be serious and widespread problems. Children were vulnerable to child abuse in all settings: home, community, school, residential institutions, and the workplace. Of the 805 reported incidents of rape against women and girls, 473 were girls. Of the 473 child victims, 39 were killed after being raped, 84 were victims of gang rape, and 10 committed suicide as a result of mental stress after the crime. Local human rights groups reported numerous rapes and rape attempts against women under the age of 17 during the year. On August 15, a prominent case developed when Luton Mondol of Jessore allegedly raped a 10th grade female student on her way home from class. On August 23, the girl committed suicide after the case became public. On August 25, the girl's father filed a criminal complaint against Luton and his father. Luton fled, and police arrested and jailed his father, although no charges were filed against the father.

Despite advances, including establishing a monitoring agency in the MHA, trafficking of children and providing care and protection to survivors of trafficking continued to be a problem. Child labor and abuse at the workplace remained a problem in certain industries, mostly in the informal sector, and child workers were vulnerable to all forms of abuse at their informal workplaces.

Child Marriage: The legal age of marriage is 18 for women and 21 for men, but underage marriage was a widespread problem. Reliable statistics concerning underage marriage were difficult to find because marriage and birth registrations were sporadic. The UN's *State of the World's Children 2012* report stated that between 2000 and 2010 the percentage of women between the ages of 20 and 24 who were married by the age of 18 was 66 percent and that 32 percent were married by the age of 15. In an effort to reduce child marriages, the government offered stipends for girls' school expenses beyond the compulsory eighth grade level. The government and NGOs conducted workshops and public events to teach parents the importance of waiting until their daughters were 18 to marry.

However, due to cultural and traditional beliefs and practices, the practice of early marriage continued.

Sexual Exploitation of Children: The penalty for sexual exploitation of children is 10 years to life imprisonment. As defined by the Women and Children's Repression Prevention Act, the minimum age of consent to sex is 16; however, the penal code sets the age at 14. The discrepancy has not been challenged in court. Child pornography, the selling or distributing of obscene material, is prohibited, and the Pornography Control Act passed in March sets the maximum penalty at 10 years in prison coupled with a fine of 500,000 taka (approximately $6,200). The previous penalty was three months' imprisonment. In 2009 the International Labor Organization (ILO) and the Bangladesh Bureau of Statistics completed a baseline survey on commercial sexual exploitation of children. According to the survey, of 18,902 child victims of sexual exploitation, 83 percent were girls, 9 percent were transgender children, and 8 percent were boys. The survey reported that 40 percent of the girls and 53 percent of the boys were under the age of 16.

International Child Abductions: The country is not a party to the 1980 Hague Convention on the Civil Aspects of International Child Abduction.

Anti-Semitism

There was no Jewish community in the country, and there were no reports of anti- Semitic acts, but some newspapers occasionally printed anti-Semitic articles and commentary.

Trafficking in Persons

See the State Department's *Trafficking in Persons Report* at www.state.gov/j/tip.

Persons with Disabilities

The law provides for equal treatment and freedom from discrimination for persons with disabilities; however, persons with disabilities faced social and economic discrimination. The law focuses on prevention of disability, treatment, education, rehabilitation, employment, transport accessibility, and advocacy.

The law's effect was limited due to vague obligations, a weak implementation mechanism, and a sweeping indemnity clause. Most provisions create positive obligations, which were difficult to enforce. For example, the obligation on the government to provide persons with disabilities free education until the age of 18 has not been translated into tangible results. The law exempts all government employees from prosecution, limiting enforcement. The law provides inadequate safeguards against involuntary institutionalization and minimal oversight of guardians and caregivers.

The NGO Action against Disability estimated that there were 16 million persons with disabilities, or 10 percent of the population. The government estimated a lower figure of 1.5 to 2 percent of the population.

The law excludes children with "mental deficiency" from compulsory public education. According to Action against Disability, 90 percent of children with disabilities are barred from attending public school. The government trained teachers on inclusive education and recruited disability specialists at the district level. The government also allocated stipends for 19,000 students with disabilities. Additionally, the government began a vocational skills training program for persons with disabilities.

In March the high court ruled that persons with disabilities could take the Bangladesh Civil Service examinations. Persons with disabilities had previously been barred from applying for civil or judicial service positions.

The law contains extensive accessibility requirements for new buildings. In practice, however, authorities approved construction plans for new buildings without close compliance with these requirements.

The law afforded persons with disabilities the same access to information rights as those without disabilities, but family and community dynamics often influenced whether or not these rights were exercised.

The law identifies persons with disabilities as a priority group for government- sponsored legal services. The Ministry of Social Welfare, Department of Social Services, and National Foundation for the Development of the Disabled are the government agencies responsible for protecting the rights of persons with disabilities. Due to inaccessibility and discrimination, persons with disabilities were sometimes excluded from mainstream government health, education, and social protective services. The government reduced taxes on several hundred items designed to assist persons with disabilities.

Government facilities for treating persons with mental disabilities were inadequate. The Ministry of Health established child development centers in all public medical colleges to assess neurological disabilities. Several private initiatives existed for medical and vocational rehabilitation as well as for employment of persons with disabilities. National and international NGOs provided services and advocated for persons with disabilities. The government also promoted autism research and awareness.

National/Racial/Ethnic Minorities

On September 29 and 30, communal attacks occurred against more than 100 Buddhist homes, temples, and monasteries in the Cox's Bazar district. The prime minister and home minister strongly condemned the violence and pledged to find the perpetrators. By October 11, police had arrested 284 persons in connection with the violence. On November 8, the MHA released the report of its official investigative body on the attacks, which stated that the violence was planned at least 10 days in advance, implicated 205 persons, and cited local law enforcement's failure to act promptly and swiftly. The report blamed then superintendent of police of Cox's Bazar Selim Md Jahangir and then officer in charge of the Ramu police station AK Nazibul Islam for failing to take appropriate measures and for neglecting their official duties. Both officers were withdrawn from their duty stations and assigned elsewhere.

Indigenous People

The indigenous community experienced widespread discrimination and abuses, despite government quotas for indigenous participation in the civil service and higher education as called for in the 1997 Peace Accord. Indigenous people were unable to participate effectively in decisions affecting their lands due to disagreements regarding the structure and policies of the land commission. Strict security measures prevented some indigenous people and activists' efforts to combat discrimination.

Indigenous people also suffered from societal violence. According to Odhikar, clashes between ethnic Bengali settlers and members of the indigenous community, as well as other forms of violence, led to 30 deaths, 78 injuries, and 15 rapes. The largest instance of societal violence against the indigenous community occurred in Rangamati on September 22, when rioters injured 50 to 100 individuals and looted stores, homes, and marketplaces. Law enforcement officials stopped the violence and banned public gatherings, shut offices, and banned vehicle traffic for two days. The government called a committee of inquiry into the attack, but at year's end had not released any information about the perpetrators. The committee recommended exemplary punishment for those responsible and made several recommendations to maintain peace in the town. The committee concluded that the incident occurred due to lack of trust between the indigenous and Bengali communities and urged full implementation of the Peace Accord.

The indigenous community was restricted from practicing its culture and traditions. The government does not officially recognize the presence of indigenous people in the country, calling them instead "small ethnic groups." On March 11, in a letter to local officials in anticipation of World Indigenous Day on August 9, the Ministry of Local Governance and Rural Development called it an "unnecessary celebration program" and ordered officials to broadcast that there were no indigenous people in the country. Indigenous people were prohibited from observing the day, which in the past included music, seminars, fairs, and rallies.

Indigenous groups and NGOs reported increased monitoring by civilian and military intelligence agencies. The CHT Commission, an international private group that worked to implement the Peace Accord, reported constant physical surveillance during its visit to the Bandarban district in January, which prevented it from conducting private meetings. Authorities evicted three foreigners from the CHT for "suspicious activities," such as speaking with journalists and visiting development projects.

The central government retained authority over land use. The land commission, designed to investigate and return all illegally acquired land, did not resolve any disputes throughout the year, as Bengalis and indigenous people questioned the structure and impartiality of the commission.

Indigenous communities in areas other than the Hill Tracts reported the loss of land to Bengali Muslims. The government did not curtail work on land traditionally owned by indigenous communities in the Moulvibazar and Modhupur forest areas, nor did it undertake any new activities. Indigenous communities, local human rights organizations, and churches in those areas claimed that the government had yet to withdraw thousands of false charges that the Forestry Department had filed against indigenous residents.

Societal Abuses, Discrimination, and Acts of Violence Based on Sexual Orientation and Gender Identity

Consensual same-sex sexual activity is illegal, but the law was not enforced. Lesbian, gay, bisexual, and transgender (LGBT) groups reported that police used the law as a pretext to bully LGBT individuals, particularly those seen as effeminate men. There were several informal support networks for gays, but organizations to assist lesbians were rare. Gays and lesbians often faced strong family pressure to marry opposite-sex partners.

Attacks on LGBT persons occurred on occasion, but those offenses were difficult to document because victims desired confidentiality. The Bandhu Social Welfare Society, a local NGO, reported 137 cases of assault against LGBT persons during the year, as compared with 109 in 2011. Strong social stigma based on sexual orientation was common and prevented open discussion of the subject.

The Ministries of Public Administration and Education conducted a pilot project to help integrate transgender persons into mainstream society. The project gave transgender persons 90 days of job skills training, began an awareness program to change negative views of the community, and established a foundation for transgender persons to continue the program.

On June 21, Nobel Peace Prize laureate Mohammad Yunus publicly expressed solidarity with LGBT individuals and condemned violence against them in a joint statement with three other Nobel laureates. The statement acknowledged the legacy of colonial-era legislation and called the criminalization of adult, consensual same sex activity unacceptable.

Other Societal Violence or Discrimination

Vigilante killings occurred during the year, and reports from rights organizations and the media suggested that the problem increased compared with 2010. Odhikar reported at least 132 killings through mob justice, but local human rights organizations acknowledged that the number of reported cases probably represented only a fraction of the actual incidents. One prominent abuse case was that of Mamun Bhuiyan from Kaliganj, Gazipur, who died on May 29 after being beaten by rivals. After an investigation, the MHA concluded that Bhuiyan's rivals killed him in front of police after taking him from police custody.

Illegal fatwas and village arbitration, which Odhikar defined as rulings given by community leaders rather than religious scholars, also occurred. Odhikar reported 17 such cases throughout the year against both men and women.

There were no reported cases of violence or discrimination against HIV/AIDS patients. NGOs believed that this was partly a function of the refusal of victims to identify themselves and an absence of research due to the relatively low rate of HIV/AIDS in the country.

SECTION 7. WORKER RIGHTS

a. Freedom of Association and the Right to Collective Bargaining

The law provides for the protection of the right to join unions and, with government approval, the right to form a union, although numerous restrictions on union registration remained. For example, the law requires more than 30 percent of an enterprise's total workforce to be members before approval can be granted, and the union can be dissolved if membership falls below 30 percent. In addition, no more than three trade unions can be registered in any establishment, and managerial staff, firefighting staff, security guards, and other employees designated by employers as "confidential" may not join a union. Civil service and security force employees are legally prohibited from forming unions.

The registrar of trade unions may deregister unions with the approval of a labor court, and during the year some unions were deregistered for violations of the law.

The law affords unions the right of appeal in the case of dissolution or denial of registration.

The law recognizes the right to strike but with many limitations. For example, 75 percent of union members must consent to a strike before it can proceed. The government can terminate any strike lasting more than 30 days and refer the matter to labor courts for adjudication. The law additionally prohibits strikes for the first three years of commercial production or if the factory was built with foreign investment or owned by a foreign investor.

The law includes provisions protecting unions from employer interference in organizing activities; however, employers, particularly in the ready-made garment industry, often sought to curtail this right. The law requires every factory to have a participation committee, but the Ministry of Labor reported there were no such committees in approximately 40 percent of factories.

Under the law, legally registered unions are entitled to bargain collectively with employers; however, this was rarely implemented. Labor organizations reported that in some companies workers feared reprisals and did not exercise their collective bargaining rights.

The law establishes mechanisms for conciliation, arbitration, and dispute resolution by a labor court. Workers in a collective-bargaining union have the right to strike in the event of a failure to reach a settlement. Civil servants and security forces do not have recourse to mechanisms for conciliation, arbitration, and labor court resolution; however, they may avail themselves of the government service regulation and file cases in a specified court, such as an administrative tribunal. In practice few strikes followed the cumbersome legal requirements, and strikes or walkouts often occurred spontaneously.

The director of labor rules on discrimination complaints involving union organizing activities except those in export processing zones (EPZs). Union activists alleged that the Ministry of Labor shared lists of union supporters with enterprises, leading to antiunion firings. A labor court can order the reinstatement of workers fired for union activities. However, due to a large backlog of unresolved cases, no workers received reinstatement orders during the year. Odhikar reported that 2,712 garment workers were terminated for demanding increased wages, overtime payment, customary holiday bonuses, or punishment of factory staff accused of harassing workers.

The law specifies association rights in the EPZs. Welfare associations provided for by the law are afforded many of the same basic powers as unions, including the right to engage in collective bargaining. Under the law a labor court functions as the EPZ labor tribunal, and EPZ workers can file complaints to enforce broader legal rights in the EPZs. Welfare associations are prohibited, however, from establishing any connection to outside political parties or NGOs, and the law prohibits strikes until October 31, 2013.

Many workers associations in EPZ factories were not formally registered because factory managers discouraged employees attempting to organize associations. Some factory managers strongly discouraged workers from meeting with outside labor organizations and sometimes terminated workers who did. The Bangladesh EPZ Authority failed to provide effective measures to allow the formation of federations of workers.

EPZ factory officials interpreted EPZ regulations and applicable laws narrowly and claimed they were exempted from the broader labor law. Labor groups challenged this claim. Workers' legal cases against EPZ factories that did not follow the law remained unresolved at year's end.

Factory workers in the garment industry who held protests to demand increased wages were generally met by riot police. In June garments workers protested for 10 days in Ashulia, demanding a wage increase to keep up with inflation and higher food prices. The Bangladesh Garments Manufacturers and Exporters Association closed 300 factories during the unrest. The Ministry of Labor formed a crisis management committee that mediated a solution by offering food subsidies to workers.

Labor organizers reported acts of intimidation and abuse, arbitrary lockouts, firing of employees, and increased scrutiny by security forces and the NSI. Authorities sometimes arrested labor organizers for destruction of property and other charges, in what some NGOs considered repression of labor rights activists.

On April 4, Aminul Islam, an organizer for the Bangladesh Garments and Industrial Workers Federation (BGIWF) and staff member of the BCWS disappeared from Savar in Dhaka division and was found dead on April 8 in Ghatail, Tangail. Media reports indicated his body showed signs of torture. The government's investigation suggested that Aminul might have been killed due to his union-organizing activities. The primary suspect in the case, Mustafiz, may have been an informant for the NSI and has not been seen since Aminul's death. As of the end of the year, no charges had been filed.

BCWS leaders continued to face criminal charges for participating in demonstrations in 2010 for increased wages. The government dropped charges in one case two-and-a-half years after its filing. Another 10 cases remained outstanding against labor federation leaders at year's end. The BCWS remained deregistered because the government would not approve its application.

Implementation of the collective bargaining law's provisions was uneven, and many private sector employers discouraged union activity or terminated workers after forming unions. Labor rights NGOs alleged that terminated union members were unable to find work in the sector because they had been blacklisted.

The Bangladesh Export Processing Zone Association (BEPZA) obstructed the rights of workers in the Rosita Knitwear and Megatex Knitters factories in the Ishwardi EPZ. After a workers' demonstration on January 30, factory owners terminated 291 workers, including the elected presidents of the welfare associations. The workers and buyers successfully negotiated the workers' reinstatement, but the BEPZA did not allow their reemployment. The BEPZA asserted that there were no regulations to require reinstatement of workers and no precedent for reemployment, notwithstanding that workers of Ringshine Textiles were reinstated at a Dhaka EPZ factory in 2006.

b. Prohibition of Forced or Compulsory Labor

The law prohibits all forms of forced or bonded labor; however, the prescribed penalty of imprisonment for up to one year or a fine was not sufficiently stringent to deter violations, and the government did not enforce the law effectively. Inspection mechanisms that enforced laws against forced labor did not function effectively.

Some men recruited to work overseas with fraudulent employment offers were subsequently exploited abroad under conditions of forced labor or debt bondage. The law does not include a specific prohibition on fraudulent recruitment, but it cites the concept of fraud as a possible element of human trafficking.

Although relatively uncommon in urban areas, there were instances of bonded labor in rural areas and in domestic service. Children and adults were forced into domestic servitude and bonded labor that involved restricted movement, nonpayment of wages, threats, and physical or sexual abuse. On February 20, the government passed a comprehensive antitrafficking law, which codified forced labor as trafficking and expanded the definition of trafficking to include labor trafficking of men and boys. The MHA chaired an interagency committee to implement a two-year National Plan of Action to combat trafficking. Traffickers are subject to life imprisonment plus a fine of 500,000 taka (approximately $6,200). The law also provides that victims of forced labor have access to shelter and other protective services afforded to trafficking victims.

Also see the Department of State's *Trafficking in Persons Report* at www.state.gov/j/tip.

c. Prohibition of Child Labor and Minimum Age for Employment

By law every child must attend school through the age of 10, but there was no effective legal mechanism to enforce this provision, and child labor was widespread. The law regulates child employment, depending on the type of work and the child's age. The minimum age for work is 14, and the minimum age for hazardous work is 18. The law allows for certain exceptions, permitting children who are 12 or 13 to perform restricted forms of light work. The law specifies penalties for child labor violations, typically nominal fines of less than 5,000 taka ($62).

The ILO estimated that 3.7 million children worked and that 1.3 million worked in hazardous sectors.

Children frequently worked in the informal sector in areas including the road transport industry, manufacturing, and the service industry. Children also worked in such hazardous activities as stone breaking, dyeing operations, blacksmith assistance, and construction. Forced child labor was present in the fish-drying industry, which exposed them to harmful chemicals, dangerous machines, and long hours of work. In urban areas street children engaged in work, such as begging, working as porters, shining shoes, collecting paper, and selling flowers. These children were vulnerable to exploitation, for example to engage in smuggling or selling drugs.

Children routinely performed domestic work. The government occasionally brought criminal charges against employers who abused domestic servants.

The Ministry of Labor's enforcement mechanisms were insufficient for the large, urban informal sector, and there was little enforcement of child labor laws outside the export garment and shrimp-processing sectors. Agriculture and other informal sectors that had no government oversight employed large numbers of children.

The Child Labor Unit in the Ministry of Labor and Employment monitored, coordinated, and supervised child labor programs. In 2011 the Child Labor Unit developed a Child Labor Monitoring Information System to manage child labor- related data collected by different ministries. The government also developed a national program to eliminate the worst forms of child labor by 2015. The program includes monitoring workplaces and education for children and their families.

Also see the Department of Labor's *Findings on the Worst Forms of Child Labor* at www.dol.gov/ilab/programs/ocft/tda.htm.

d. Acceptable Conditions of Work

For the five-year period 2007-12, the National Minimum Wage Board (NMWB) established the minimum monthly wage at 1,500 taka ($19) for all economic sectors not covered by industry-specific wages. The NMWB may convene at any time, but it must meet every five years in a tripartite forum to set wage structures and benefits industry by industry. In the garment industry the Ministry of Labor raised the minimum wage in 2010 from 1,662 taka ($21) per month to 3,000 taka ($37) per month. Wages were sometimes higher than the minimum wage, and wages in the EPZs were typically higher than general wage levels. None of the set minimum wages provided a sufficient standard of living for urban dwellers. The International Food Policy Research Institute estimated the national poverty income level to be 1,487 taka ($18) per capita per month. There was no mechanism to keep the minimum wage in line with inflation, which averaged 10 percent since the wage was last increased in 2010. By law a standard workday is eight hours. A standard workweek is 48 hours but can be extended to 60 hours, subject to the payment of an overtime allowance that is double the basic wage. The average workweek should not exceed 56 hours. Workers must have one hour of rest if they work for more than six hours a day, a half-hour of rest for more than five hours a day, and one hour's rest at intervals for more than eight hours' work in a day. Factory workers receive one day off every week. Shop workers receive one-and-a-half days off per week.

In practice these legal limits were routinely violated, and enforcement of the law was weak. In the ready-made garment sector, employers often required workers to labor 12 hours a day or more to meet export deadlines, but they did not always properly compensate workers for their time. Employers commonly delayed workers' pay or denied full leave benefits.

The law establishes occupational health and safety standards. Workers' groups stated that the standards established by law were sufficient but that they were not routinely enforced. Workers can invoke legal mechanisms to enforce the law but did so in few cases. Enforcement by the Labor Ministry's industrial inspectors was weak due to the low number of labor inspectors. There were 91 inspectors nationwide, of whom approximately 52 worked in the factories division; 92 inspector positions remained vacant. Inspections were unannounced, but in practice inspectors sometimes notified factory owners. The law provides for a maximum fine of 25,000 taka (approximately $309) for noncompliance, but this did not deter violations.

Safety conditions at many workplaces were extremely poor. Because of high unemployment rates and inadequate enforcement of laws, workers who demanded redress for dangerous working conditions or who refused to work under hazardous conditions risked losing their jobs. On November 24, a factory fire at Tazreen Fashions Ltd. killed at least 110 workers. The fire department stated that an electrical short circuit likely caused the fire, but poor management contributed to the high death toll. Victims stated their managers locked one exit route and told workers that the fire alarm was false, thereby delaying timely evacuation. The incident exposed weak safety regulations in the garments sector, as the factory building also lacked an external fire escape route, emergency lighting in the work area, and a sprinkler system.

On October 9, HRW reported on labor conditions in 150 tanneries in Dhaka's Hazaribagh neighborhood. The report claimed that tanneries mistreated workers with impunity, since the government did not enforce labor laws there. HRW researchers found instances of child labor, worker exposure to toxic chemicals without the use of protective gear, and frequent life-threatening injuries due to operating dangerous machinery.

On April 23, the Solidarity Center and Social Activities for Environment released a joint report on inadequate health and safety protections in the shrimp-processing industry. Nearly three-quarters of the workers surveyed for the report stated that they received payments below the minimum wage. The majority of workers surveyed did not have an employment contract. Women reported earning less than men for the same work, and only eight of 145 shrimp factories reportedly had unions. No reliable labor statistics were available on the large informal sector in which the majority of citizens worked, and it was difficult to enforce labor laws in the sector. The ILO reported that 47.3 million of the 56.7 million workers in the country were employed in the informal sector.

In: Bangladesh
Editor: Gregory P. Davis

ISBN: 978-1-63117-003-4

Chapter 4

BANGLADESH 2012 INTERNATIONAL RELIGIOUS FREEDOM REPORT*

U.S. Department of State,
Bureau of Democracy, Human Rights and Labor

EXECUTIVE SUMMARY

The constitution and other laws and policies protect religious freedom and, in practice, the government generally respected religious freedom. The trend in the government's respect for religious freedom did not change significantly during the year. The government made limited progress on the long-standing issue of returning "vested property" to Hindus dating from the country's liberation war, and also took steps towards equalizing family law for Hindus through legislating optional marriage registration. The constitution states that Islam is the state religion, but reaffirms the nation is a secular state that "shall ensure equal status and equal right in the practice of the Hindu, Buddhist, Christian, and other religions." The constitution provides for the right to profess, practice, or propagate all religions, subject to law, public order, and morality. Although government officials, including police, were sometimes slow to assist members of minority religious groups who were

* This document was released by the U.S. Department of State; Bureau of Democracy, Human Rights and Labor, May 2013.

victims of harassment and violence, there were examples of timely and effective police intervention.

There were reports of societal abuses and discrimination based on religious affiliation, belief, or practice. There were scattered attacks on members of minority religious and ethnic groups, most notably against Buddhists in Ramu in September and October. Most attacks consisted of arson and looting of religious sites and homes. Because many members of minority religious groups also had low economic and social status, they were often seen as having little political recourse. Members of Hindu, Christian, Buddhist, and Ahmadiyya Muslim minority groups experienced harassment and sometimes violence from the Sunni Muslim majority population. The government and many civil society leaders stated that violence against members of minority religious groups normally had political or economic dimensions, and could not be attributed solely to religious belief or affiliation.

In meetings with officials and in public statements, the U.S. embassy encouraged the government to protect the rights of members of minority religious groups. The embassy denounced acts of religious intolerance publicly and privately, and called on the government to ensure due process for all citizens. U.S. development programs in the country supported religious tolerance.

Section I. Religious Demography

According to the 2011 census, Sunni Muslims constitute 90 percent of the population and Hindus make up 9.5 percent of a total population of 152.5 million. The remainder of the population is predominantly Christian (mostly Roman Catholic) and Theravada-Hinayana Buddhist. Ethnic and religious minority groups often overlap and are concentrated in the Chittagong Hill Tracts and northern districts. Buddhists are predominantly found among the indigenous (non-Bengali) populations of the Chittagong Hill Tracts. Bengali and ethnic minority Christians live in communities across the country, concentrating in Barisal City, Gournadi in Barisal District, Baniarchar in Gopalganj, Monipuripara in Dhaka, Christianpara in Mohakhal, Nagori in Gazipur, and Khulna City. There also are small populations of Shia Muslims, Bahais, animists, and Ahmadiyya Muslims. Estimates of their numbers varied from a few thousand to 100,000 adherents per group.

Most noncitizen residents are of Bangladeshi descent and practice Islam. Separately, there are approximately 30,000 registered Rohingya refugees and between 250,000 and 450,000 unregistered Rohingya practicing Islam in the southeast around Cox's Bazar.

SECTION II. STATUS OF GOVERNMENT RESPECT FOR RELIGIOUS FREEDOM

Legal/Policy Framework

The constitution and other laws and policies protect religious freedom. The constitution provides for the right to profess, practice, or propagate all religions, subject to law, public order, and morality. While Islam is the state religion, the constitution affirms that the country is a secular state. Family law has separate provisions for Muslims, Hindus, and Christians.

An amendment to the constitution, upheld by the Supreme Court in 2010, bans unions, associations, or parties based on religion. Despite this nominal ban, religious parties continue to play an active role in the country's politics, and authorities do not enforce the ban.

Under the penal code, statements or acts made with a "deliberate and malicious" intent to insult religious sentiments are subject to fines or up to two years in prison. In addition, the Code of Criminal Procedure states, "The government may confiscate all copies of a newspaper if it publishes anything that creates enmity and hatred among the citizens or denigrates religious beliefs."

Islamic law plays some role in civil matters pertaining to the Muslim community; however, there is no formal implementation of Islamic law, and it is not imposed on non-Muslims. Alternative dispute resolution is available to individuals for settling family arguments and other civil matters not related to land ownership. With the consent of both parties, arbitrators rely on principles found in Islamic law for settling disputes.

Family laws concerning marriage, divorce, and adoption differ slightly depending on the religious beliefs of the persons involved. Muslim and Hindu family laws are codified in the legal system. For example, a Muslim man may marry as many as four wives, although he must get his first wife's signed permission before marrying an additional woman. Society strongly discourages polygamy, and Muslims rarely practice it. A Christian man may marry only one woman. Under Hindu law in the country there are limited provisions for divorce, such as impotency, torture, or madness. Hindu widows can legally remarry, and marriage registration for Hindus is optional. The family law of the religion of the two parties concerned governs their marriage rituals and proceedings; however, marriages also are registered with the state. There are no legal restrictions on marriage between members of different religious groups.

Under the Muslim family ordinance, females inherit less than males, and wives have fewer divorce rights than husbands. Laws provide some protection for women against arbitrary divorce and polygamy without the consent of the first wife, but the protections generally apply only to registered marriages. In rural areas, couples occasionally do not register their marriages. Under the law, a Muslim husband is required to pay his former wife alimony for three months, but the authorities do not always enforce this requirement.

The Hindu Marriage Registration Act, passed on September 18, retains marriage registration as optional but offers additional legal and social protection to Hindus, particularly to safeguard women from financial neglect or abuse.

The Vested Property Act remained in force until 2001, allowing the government to expropriate "enemy" (in practice, Hindu) lands. Over the course of its existence, the government seized approximately 2.6 million acres of land, affecting almost all Hindus in the country. Many Hindus continued efforts to recover land lost under the act. The Vested Properties Return (Amendment) Bill of 2011 obligates the government to publish lists of returnable vested property through gazette notification within 120 days. Subsequently, Hindu leaders submitted applications to reclaim previously seized vested property and requested an extension to prepare further applications. The Vested Property Return (Second Amendment) Act of 2012, passed on September 18, gives an additional 180 days for interested parties to submit applications for adjudication.

The government does not require non-Muslim religious groups to register, but all nongovernmental organizations (NGOs), including religiously affiliated ones, must register with the government's NGO Affairs Bureau if they receive foreign financial assistance for social development projects.

Religious studies are part of the curriculum in government schools. Students attend classes in which their own religious beliefs are taught. Schools with few students from minority religious groups often make arrangements with local churches or temples to hold religious studies classes outside school hours.

There are an estimated 46,000 madrassahs. Approximately 2 percent of primary school students in rural areas attend "Qaumi" madrassahs, independent private madrassahs not regulated by the government, according to a 2009 World Bank study. The same study estimates another 8 percent of primary school students and 19 percent of secondary school students attend "Aliyah" madrassahs, state-regulated private madrassahs teaching a government-approved curriculum. Other primary school students attend "Forkania" madrassahs attached to mosques, and some students in urban areas attend "Cadet" madrassahs, which blend religious and non-religious studies. The rest either attend secular government schools or NGOrun schools, or did not attend school. There are no known government-run Christian, Hindu, or Buddhist schools, although there are private religious schools throughout the country.

The government observes the following religious holidays as national holidays: Eid Milad un-Nabi, Shab-e-Barat, Shab-e-Qadar, Jumatul Wida, Eid Ul Fitr, Eid Ul Azha, Muharram; Krishna Janmashtami; Durga Puja; Buddha Purnima; and Christmas.

Government Practices

There were no reports of abuses of religious freedom. Government institutions and the courts generally protected religious freedom. However, some government practices restricted members of minority religious groups.

There were no legal hiring preferences for government jobs based on religious beliefs. In contrast to previous years, there were no reports of members of minority religious groups being disadvantaged in access to military or government jobs. In the cabinet, five of 51 ministers were non-Muslim, including two Buddhists, two Hindus, and a Christian. While there were numerous members of minority groups in the higher ranks of government, no official statistics existed to determine to what extent the proportion corresponded with their proportion in the population. Although employees were not required to disclose their religious affiliation, it could generally be determined by a person's name.

The government routinely posted law enforcement personnel at religious festivals and events considered at risk of being targets for extremists. Through additional security deployments and public statements, the government promoted the peaceful celebration of Hindu, Christian, Buddhist, and secular Bengali festivals. Durga Puja, Christmas, Easter, Buddha Purnima, and Pohela Boisakh (Bengali New Year) all received government support of this kind.

The government continued to block Facebook pages it deemed offensive for religious reasons.

The constitution provides for the right to promulgate the religion of one's choice, but local authorities and communities often objected to efforts to convert persons from Islam, which led to heightened government interest in the activities of certain Christian groups.

On May 12, the Supreme Court's appellate division overturned a 2001 high court ruling banning fatwas; however, the court declared that fatwas could be used only to settle religious matters and could not be invoked to justify meting out punishment, nor could they supersede existing secular law Islamic tradition. Islamic tradition dictated that only muftis with expertise in Islamic law could declare a fatwa. Despite these restrictions, village religious leaders sometimes made declarations they described as fatwas. Such declarations resulted in extrajudicial punishments, often against women, for perceived moral transgressions.

The government operated training academies for imams and proclaimed Islamic festival days, but generally did not dictate sermon content or select or pay clergy. However, the government had the authority to appoint or remove imams, and exercised some indirect influence over sermon content in government mosques, including in the national mosque, Baitul Mukarram. The government monitored the content of religious education in madrassahs.

The Ministry of Religious Affairs administered four funds for religious and cultural activities: the Islamic Foundation, the Hindu Welfare Trust, the Christian Religious Welfare Trust, and the Buddhist Welfare Trust. These religious trusts used their funding for literacy and religious programs, observing festivals, repairing religious buildings, and for helping destitute families.

SECTION III. STATUS OF SOCIETAL RESPECT FOR RELIGIOUS FREEDOM

There were reports of societal abuses or discrimination based on religious affiliation, belief, or practice, and prominent societal leaders took positive steps to promote religious freedom. Violence directed against members of minority religious groups continued to result in the loss of lives and property, but it was difficult to determine whether the true motives were religious animosity, criminal intent, personal conflict, property disputes, or some combination thereof. Members of minority religious groups were often at the bottom of the social hierarchy and had the least political recourse.

Societal groups at times incited violence against or harassment of members of minority religious groups. The most common type of abuse was arson and looting of religious sites and homes. For example, on April 3, Muslim students from Fatehpur, Satkhira looted and burned eight Hindu families' homes, including the home of the local school superintendent. The Fatehpur incident occurred after high school students performed a play which allegedly insulted the Prophet Mohammed. On August 4 in Chirirbandar, Dinajpur, a local Muslim official told journalists that Hindus opposed building a mosque on donated land. Fearing violence, the police banned public gatherings, but were overwhelmed by a crowd of 1,500 largely Muslim community members who burned at least 20 homes, affecting 35 Hindu families. Police arrested eight people in connection with the arson, and suspended construction of the mosque.

Buddhists in Ramu, Cox's Bazar, and neighboring cities experienced communal violence on September 29 and 30. After rumors spread that a local Buddhist youth posted anti-Islamic photos on Facebook, thousands of protesters burned and vandalized Buddhist homes and temples. Local police called in supplemental security forces to quell the violence, but attackers had already set fire to at least 15 Buddhist temples and 100 homes. The Home Ministry increased law enforcement presence around neighboring Buddhist sites. Violence spread in the following days to Patiya, Chittagong, where two Buddhist monasteries and one Hindu temple were burned, and to Ukhia and Teknaf, Cox's Bazar, where two monasteries and five homes were burned. The prime minister, home minister, and foreign minister all immediately issued strong statements condemning the violence and reaffirming the tolerant, secular, multi-religious nature of the country. The prime minister travelled to Ramu to convey the extent of her concern.

The government funded reconstruction of the burned temples and monasteries. Prominent societal leaders from all religious groups, universities, and rights organizations condemned the attack and called for interreligious harmony. According to the government's official inquiry into the Ramu incidents, the then-superintendent of police of Cox's Bazar and the then-officer-in-charge of Ramu police station failed to take appropriate measures to stop the violence. The report charged the two officials with negligence of official duties and withdrew them from their duty stations.

While contentious issues in the Hill Tracts related primarily to economic matters, including tension over increased Bengali settlement, the issues sometimes acquired an ethnic and religious tinge because many of the original inhabitants were members of tribal groups with Buddhist, Hindu, or Christian affiliation.

The Ahmadiyya Muslim community also suffered harassment. In addition to destruction of Ahmadi homes and mosques, the community faced obstacles in conducting burials and building mosques. For example, when an Ahmadi family tried to bury a family member at an ancestral site in Tejgaon, Dhaka on July 20, members of the anti-Ahmadi Khatme Nabuwat Movement obstructed his burial. When the family buried him at a different site, members of the same movement tried to exhume his body, although local officials and police stopped the exhumation attempt. On November 7, inhabitants of Taraganj, Rangpur attacked an Ahmadi community, setting fire to two homes and a mosque and injuring 15. The attackers, who numbered over 1,000, were allegedly incited by loudspeaker announcements concerning the building of a new Ahmadi mosque in the area. Police quelled the violence and arrested eleven people in connection with the attack.

Some newspapers occasionally printed anti-Semitic articles and commentary.

SECTION IV. U.S. GOVERNMENT POLICY

The U.S. embassy continued to express concern about the rights of members of religious and ethnic minorities, including in discussions with government officials. The ambassador and embassy staff traveled throughout the country and met with members of minority religious groups to discuss religious freedom concerns and demonstrate support. Embassy staff also met with local government officials, civil society members, NGOs, and local religious leaders to discuss specific cases. The ambassador and embassy officials also encouraged law enforcement to protect the rights of members of minority religious groups.

The U.S. government continued to make religious freedom, especially the problems facing the minority populations in the Chittagong Hill Tracts, a topic of discussion in meetings with government officials. Embassy officers met with representatives of organizations from the Hill Tracts and with senior government officials to relay concerns about the treatment of minorities.

Embassy officials assisted U.S. faith-based relief organizations in filing documents for approval of schools and other projects. The government was willing to discuss these subjects with U.S. officials and was helpful in resolving problems.

The ambassador hosted an interfaith iftar and another event for Christmas, both with government officials and religious leaders. His remarks on both occasions stressed the importance of continuing the country's secular and tolerant national character. Official embassy representation at Durga Puja, Buddha Purnima, and local Christmas celebrations underscored the embassy's support for minority religious groups.

The U.S. government offered programs to madrassah students and teachers on religious tolerance, human rights, and gender equality, among other topics. The embassy reached out to influential leaders nationwide, including religious leaders, to introduce the concepts and practices of modern development and democracy through training. Over 400 madrassah students and 1,100 teachers participated in programs promoting the values of diversity and tolerance, including religious tolerance, across communities in the country.

Democracy and governance projects supported by the U.S. government included religious tolerance and minority rights components.

In: Bangladesh
Editor: Gregory P. Davis

ISBN: 978-1-63117-003-4

Chapter 5

2013 INVESTMENT CLIMATE STATEMENT: BANGLADESH*

Bureau of Economic and Business Affairs

OPENNESS TO, AND RESTRICTIONS UPON, FOREIGN INVESTMENT

With a highly competitive labor force, an entrepreneurial business community and a resilient and steadily growing economy, Bangladesh offers promising opportunities for investment, especially in the energy, power, pharmaceutical, information technology and infrastructure sectors and in labor-intensive industries such as ready made garments and household textiles. The Government of Bangladesh actively seeks foreign investment, particularly in energy, power and infrastructure projects. It offers a range of investment incentives under its industrial policy and export-oriented growth strategy, with few formal distinctions between foreign and domestic private investors.

According to the 2012 World Investment Report, Bangladesh received $ 1.13 billion in foreign direct investment in FY12. This represented a 24% increase from the previous financial year, but a nominal amount compared to the $38.9 billion in foreign investment that the entire South Asia region attracted and the traditionally far larger flows that have driven export-led

* This is an edited, reformatted and augmented version of a Bureau of Economic and Business Affairs publication, dated February 2013.

growth in neighboring East Asia. Bangladesh has made gradual progress in reducing some constraints on investment, but inadequate infrastructure, financial constraints, bureaucratic delays and corruption continue to hinder foreign investment. The lack of effective judiciary or alternative dispute resolution mechanisms impedes the enforcement of contracts and the resolution of business disputes.

The installment of the current elected government in 2009 brought greater stability for investors, who were previously reluctant to pursue projects due to risks that decisions might be reversed during the preceding 2006-2009 period when the country experienced three different governments. The approach of national elections in 2013/2014 has raised concern that political uncertainty may hinder investments as continuing disagreement over the institutional mechanism for elections increases the risk of general strikes and street demonstrations that are disruptive to businesses.

Energy and Infrastructure Development

The Government of Bangladesh (GOB) has pursued ambitious plans for infrastructure development, particularly in the power sector, where it pledged to double generation capacity from 6,000 MW to 12,000 MW by 2015 and to 20,000 MW by 2020. In 2009, the government launched an initiative with modest funding for public private partnerships (PPP) and began to develop a legal and regulatory framework to implement this initiative. In 2010, due to critical power shortages and chronic delays in implementing power projects, the GOB amended procurement requirements to allow unsolicited bids and expedited the approval of power generation projects. It also aims to formulate a coal policy to encourage investment in developing coal resources and coal-based power projects. Administrative approval of the production plan of a foreign-owned, open-cast coal mine in northwest Bangladesh has remained pending since November 2005 due to local opposition and political pressure from civil society groups. The government has improved the efficiency of the main seaport in Chittagong and is constructing a four-lane highway to connect Chittagong with the capital city of Dhaka. Prolonged and contentious public procurement processes, however, continue to challenge GOB efforts to develop infrastructure projects. The landmark $ 3.1 billion Padma Bridge project, which will substantially improve interregional connectivity, has been delayed due to the World Bank's concern about transparency in the procurement process.

Legal Framework

Major laws affecting foreign investment include: the Foreign Private Investment (Promotion and Protection) Act of 1980; the Industrial Policy Act of 2005, the Bangladesh Export Processing Zones Authority Act of 1980; the Companies Act of 1994, and the Telecommunications Act of 2001. Legislation offers incentives for investors, including: 100% foreign ownership in most sectors, tax holidays and exemptions, reduced import duties on capital machinery and spare parts, and duty-free imports for 100% exporters of ready-made garments. The Government of Bangladesh extended a tax holiday scheme for start-up industries through June 30, 2013. Beneficiary industries include agro-processing, steel production, jute industries, some textile units, and telecom infrastructure except for mobile phones. A tax rebate facility to non-resident Bangladeshi investors was also extended to induce investment from abroad. Import duties and supplemental taxes remain high and constitute an important source of government revenue. Customs bonded warehouses enable companies located in EPZs to avoid duty payments on inputs for goods that will be exported. There are few performance requirements, and these do not generally impede investment. Land registration has historically been prone to disputes over competing titles, and scarcity of land is a significant investment constraint.

While discrimination against foreign investors is not widespread, the government frequently promotes local industries and some discriminatory policies and regulations exist. For example, the government has withheld approvals for imported medicines that compete with local producers and it has required majority local ownership of new shipping companies, albeit with exemptions for existing foreign-owned firms.

Investment Promotion Agencies

The Board of Investment (BOI) and the Bangladesh Export Processing Zones Authority (BEPZA) are the primary investment promotion agencies in Bangladesh. Companies must register with the BOI to obtain benefits such as tax incentives or preferential duties for imported equipment. The BOI also administers the approval of some foreign loans and payments on behalf of the Bangladesh Bank. Though the BOI is frequently touted as a one-stop shop for all investors, authority for managing foreign investment remains fragmented. The BOI can register investors in industrial projects outside the Export

Processing Zones (EPZs) and assist them with tax inquiries, land acquisition, utility hook-ups, and incorporation. The BEPZA performs the same functions for companies investing in the EPZs. Investors in infrastructure and natural resource sectors, including power, mineral resources and telecommunications must seek approval from the corresponding government ministries. Although the BOI is housed organizationally in the Prime Minister's Office, regulatory and administrative powers remain vested in the line ministries. Companies often complain that ministries require unnecessary licenses and permissions.

Currency Convertibility

Free repatriation of profits is allowed and profits are almost fully convertible on the current account; however, companies report that the procedures for repatriation of foreign currency are lengthy and cumbersome. When rising fuel imports helped swing balance of payments from surplus to deficit in 2010-2011, scarcity of foreign exchange and currency depreciation temporarily increased convertibility risks. Since 2011, the balance of payments has swung back into surplus, foreign reserves reached an all time high at the end of 2012, and convertibility risks have declined.

Privatization

The Government of Bangladesh privatized some state-owned enterprises (SOEs) during the past twenty years, but many SOEs retain an important role in the economy, particularly in the financial and energy sectors. The current government has taken steps to restructure several SOEs to improve their competitiveness. Biman Bangladesh Airline was converted into a public limited company that initiated a rebranding and fleet renewal program, including the purchase of 10 aircraft from Boeing. Three nationalized commercial banks (NCBs) -- Sonali, Janata and Agrani -- have been converted to public limited companies. Bangladesh allows private investment in power generation and natural gas exploration, but efforts to allow full foreign participation in petroleum marketing and gas distribution have stalled.

The telecommunications sector was liberalized during the last decade, leading to the development of a competitive cellular phone market. The Government has been slow to allow greater competition for international connectivity and internet telephony. In 2007, the Caretaker Government revised the International Long Distance Telecommunication Services Policy of 2007 to legalize VoIP, but the government has not yet implemented this policy.

Business Environment Indices

Measure	Year	Index/Ranking
Transparency International Corruption Index	2012	144 of 174 countries
Heritage Economic Freedom	2012	130 of 179 countries
World Bank Doing Business	2012	129 of 185 countries
MCC Government Effectiveness	2012	53rd percentile
MCC Rule of Law	2012	67th percentile
MCC Control of Corruption	2012	42nd percentile
MCC Fiscal Policy	2012	47th percentile
MCC Trade Policy	2012	4th percentile
MCC Regulatory Quality	2012	44th percentile
MCC Business Start Up	2012	76th percentile
MCC Land Rights Access	2012	22nd percentile
MCC Natural Resource Management	2012	20th percentile
MCC Access to Credit	2012	69th percentile
MCC Inflation	2012	38th percentile

Conversion and Transfer Policies

Bangladesh Bank, the central bank of Bangladesh, does not fix the exchange rate against foreign currencies, but it regulates conversion. The Bangladesh Taka is almost fully convertible for current account transactions, such as import trade and travel needs, but not for capital account transactions, such as investing, currency speculation, or e-commerce. The Foreign Investment Act guarantees the right of repatriation of invested capital, profits, capital gains, post-tax dividends, and approved royalties and fees. The central bank's exchange control regulations and the U.S.-Bangladesh Bilateral Investment Treaty (in force since 1989) provide similar investment transfer guarantees. In practice, foreign firms are able to repatriate funds, but companies report that the repatriation process is onerous and cumbersome. When balance of payment deficits contributed to temporary foreign exchange shortages in 2011, companies reported increasing delays in conversion and transfer of funds. The Board of Investment may need to approve repatriation of royalties and other fees. The Bangladesh Taka depreciated more than 15 percent against the U.S. dollar in 2011, but strengthened at the end of 2012 with overseas remittances and foreign reserves reaching record highs.

Expropriation and Compensation

Since the Foreign Investment Act of 1980 banned nationalization or expropriation without adequate compensation, the Government of Bangladesh has not nationalized or expropriated property from foreign investors. In the years immediately following independence in 1971, widespread nationalization resulted in government ownership of over 90% of fixed assets in the modern manufacturing sector, including textile, jute and sugar industries as well as all banking and insurance interests, except those in foreign (but non-Pakistani) hands. The government has since taken steps to privatize many of these industries during the last twenty years and the private sector has developed into a main driver of the country's sustained economic growth of 5-6 percent per year during the past two decades.

Dispute Settlement

A fundamental impediment to investment in Bangladesh is a weak and slow legal system in which the enforceability of contracts is uncertain. The judicial system does not provide for interest to be charged in tort judgments, thus there is no penalty for delaying proceedings. In a significant milestone, the Caretaker Government in 2007 separated the country's judiciary from the executive, but the executive has retained strong influence over the judiciary through control of judicial appointments. Reforms of other pillars of the justice system including the police, courts, and legal profession are also necessary. In lower courts, corruption is widely perceived as a serious problem. The High Court's previous reputation for impartiality has also been brought into question in recent years. Bangladeshi law allows contracts to refer dispute settlement to third country forums for resolution. Bangladesh is a signatory to the International Convention for the Settlement of Disputes (ICSID) and it acceded (on May 6, 1992) to the United Nations Convention for the Recognition and Enforcement of Foreign Arbitral Awards. Bangladesh is also a party to the South Asia Association for Regional Cooperation (SAARC) Agreement for the Establishment of an Arbitration Council, signed November

13, 2005, which aims to establish a permanent alternative dispute resolution center in one of the SAARC member countries. A provision of the U.S.-Bangladesh Bilateral Investment Treaty permits submission of investment disputes to ICSID for third-party settlement.

The ability of the Bangladeshi judicial system to enforce its own awards is weak, and there is no reason to believe that enforcement of foreign judgments would be stronger. The Bangladesh Export Promotion Bureau is sometimes helpful in facilitating dispute settlement for export-related transactions. Major Bangladeshi trade and business associations can also help to resolve transaction disputes.

Many laws affecting investment in Bangladesh are old and outdated. Bankruptcy laws, which apply mainly to individual insolvency, are not being used because of a web of falsified assets and uncollectible cross-indebtedness supporting insolvent banks and companies. A Bankruptcy Act was enacted in 1997 but has been ineffective in addressing these issues.

Dispute settlement is also hampered by shortcomings in accounting practices and in the registration of real property. With the exception of those conducted by a few internationally affiliated accounting firms, audits of balance sheets and profit and loss statements often follow clients' instructions and fail to conform to international standards. Documents affecting title to real property are often not registered, complicating transfer of ownership and collateral agreements.

Performance Requirements/Incentives

The GOB's industrial policies favor manufacturing and labor-intensive industries that use local inputs. A variety of subsidies and other incentives are available to different industrial ventures, primarily in export sectors and, to a certain extent, import substitution sectors. The Government also provides loans at concessionary rates through state banks and government-owned development banks for exports, cottage industries, and agriculture. These incentives are available to both domestic and foreign investors.

In order to simplify the tariff structure and generate more revenue through import duties, the government developed a four-tier duty structure with higher duties on finished products, but reduced duties on industrial inputs such as capital machinery, spare parts, basic raw materials, and intermediate raw materials.

The government also offers a variety of tax incentives to selected sectors of the economy, including:

- A 50% rebate for taxable income generated from export earnings;
- An income tax exemption on export earnings from handicrafts and cottage industries;
- Tax holidays of four to six years, depending on location, for new industrial enterprises in the textile, pharmaceuticals, plastic, ceramics, sanitary ware, iron, steel, fertilizer, insecticide, computer hardware, petrochemicals, pharmaceutical raw materials, agricultural equipment, and industrial machinery. (Note: This provision has been extended annually, with the current extension allowing business to begin claiming this incentive by June 2013.)
- A 10-year tax holiday for enterprises in the EPZs;
- Accelerated depreciation for enterprises not eligible for a tax holiday; and,
- Income tax exemptions for up to 15 years for power projects.

Right to Private Ownership and Establishment

Foreign and domestic private entities can establish and own, operate, and dispose of interests in most types of business enterprises. Four sectors, however, are reserved for government investment:

- arms and ammunition and other defense equipment and machinery
- forest plantation and mechanized extraction within the bounds of reserved forests
- production of nuclear energy
- security printing

Protection of Property Rights

Although land, whether for purchase or lease, is often critical for investment and as security for loans, antiquated real property laws and poor record-keeping systems can complicate land and property transactions. Land registration records have been historically prone to competing claims.

Instruments take effect from the date of execution, not the date of registration, so a bona fide purchaser can never be certain of title. Property owners can obtain mortgages, but parties avoid registering mortgages, liens, and encumbrances due to the high cost of stamp duties (i.e., transaction taxes based on property value) and other charges.

Bangladesh has slowly made progress bringing its legislative framework into compliance with the Agreement on Trade-Related Aspects of Intellectual Property Rights (TRIPS). The GOB enacted a Copyright Law in July 2000 (later amended in 2005) and a Trademarks Act in 2009, and it is preparing draft Patent and Design laws to modernize its current Patent and Design legislation dating from 1911. Once fully implemented, this legislation is intended to bring the country's intellectual property laws into full compliance with TRIPS requirements.

The government has limited resources for IPR protection. Enforcement actions against IPR violators are rare despite widespread availability of pirated goods. The government also sets a poor example by failing to account fully for software in its tenders. A number of American firms, including film studios, manufacturers of consumer goods, and software firms, have reported violations of their intellectual property rights. Bangladesh is a member of the World Intellectual Property Organization (WIPO); and acceded to the Paris Convention on Intellectual Property in 1991.

Transparency of the Regulatory System

Starting from a position of extreme over-regulation, the government has gradually moved since 1989 to decrease regulatory obstruction of private business. Although some officials have shown genuine commitment to these reforms, in general, changes encountered broad-based resistance from many groups in the economy, including influential members of the business community. The official chambers of commerce include manufacturers in protected industries and well-connected commission agents pursuing government contracts. Chamber members have called for a greater voice for the private sector in government decisions and for privatization, but at the same time many support protectionism and subsidies for their own industries.

Policy and regulations in Bangladesh are often not clear, consistent, or publicized. Generally, the civil service, businesses, professionals, trade unions, and political parties have vested interests in a system in which confidentiality is used as an excuse for lack of transparency and in which patron-client relationships are the norm. The country's poorly paid civil servants have often used registration and regulatory processes as rent-seeking opportunities. Bangladesh has made incremental progress in using information technology to improve the transparency and efficiency of some government services and developing independent agencies to regulate the energy and telecommunication sectors.

In practice, government laws, regulations and their implementation often do not reduce distortions or impediments to investment, but create them. Unhelpful treatment of businesses by some government officials, coupled with other investment climate constraints, raise startup and operational costs, add to risk, and counteract the government's praiseworthy investment incentives. The government has historically limited opportunities for the private sector to comment on proposed regulations but several agencies, including the Commerce Ministry and telecommunications regulator have posted draft legislation and regulations online and solicited input from the business community.

Efficient Capital Markets and Portfolio Investment

While Bangladesh has made gradual progress in developing capital markets, the markets have relied primarily on domestic investors with limited participation from international portfolio investors. A 2010-2011 stock market bubble and correction underscored weaknesses in capital markets and regulatory oversight. The Dhaka Stock Exchange (DSE) market capitalization rose to a peak of $48 billion in December 2010 before declining to roughly $30 billion in January 2012. A sharp increase in retail investors combined with loose monetary policy and lax regulatory oversight fueled inflation of share prices in 2010.

As steady economic growth has fueled rising domestic investment, Bangladeshi firms have increasingly relied on capital markets to finance investment projects. The DSE has attracted some foreign portfolio investors to the country's capital market; however the volume of foreign investment in Bangladesh has remained a small fraction of total market capitalization. As a result, foreign portfolio investment has had limited influence on market trends and Bangladesh's capital markets have been largely insulated from volatility of international financial markets. The government offloaded its shares of a number of State-owned Enterprises (SOEs) and government shares of various private companies in order to increase the supply of shares in the capital market.

Foreign investors have access to local credit markets, but many seek offshore financing. If they finance locally, it is usually with a foreign bank branch. Three state-owned banks, known as nationalized commercial banks (NCBs), comprise a significant portion of the banking sector's total assets. The largest NCB held assets greater than $8 billion in 2010. Financial analysts estimate that a significant share of the country's total asset base is non-performing based on their long-outstanding debts to the NCBs. The share of non-performing assets for private commercial banks ranges from two to eleven percent. The World Bank has approved a $250 million International Development Association (IDA) soft loan to Bangladesh for an ongoing enterprise growth and bank modernization project that will provide technical assistance to four NCBs.

The Securities and Exchange Commission (SEC) was formed in 1993 to regulate the DSE and CSE and protect investors. In 1997, the SEC imposed new restrictions on the involvement of foreign investors in the Bangladesh capital market. The guidelines stipulate that 10 percent of primary issues are reserved for non-resident Bangladeshis. Foreign investors have complained that this measure exacerbates a significant market drawback: the difficulty of buying or selling in volume over a reasonably short period. The SEC and the Institute of Chartered Accountants of Bangladesh have the task of enforcing reporting and audit requirements and bringing those requirements up to international standards.

Competition from State-Owned Enterprises (SOEs)

SOEs are active in banking, energy, transportation and agricultural sectors. SOEs usually report to line Ministries, though the government has allowed some increased autonomy for certain SOEs such as Biman Bangladesh Airline. State-owned banks generally maintain a wider network of branches and depositors than private banks, but private banks have gradually increased their role. Private energy companies can invest in power generation through Independent Power Purchase (IPP) agreements with the Bangladesh Power Development Board. Oil and gas firms can pursue exploration and production ventures through Production Sharing Agreements with the state-owned oil and gas company, Petrobangla. SOEs maintain control of rail transportation, but private companies compete freely in air and road transportation.

Corporate Social Responsibility (CSR)

The business community is increasingly aware and engaged in CSR activities with multinational firms and local business conglomerates leading the way. Consumers are generally less aware of CSR and there is little pressure from consumers or shareholders for companies to engage in CSR activities. While many international firms are aware of OECD guidelines and international best practices in CSR, most local firms have limited familiarity with international standards.

Political Violence

Incidents of violence targeting foreign projects or installations have generally been isolated and criminal, rather than political, in nature. Extortion of money from businesses by thugs claiming political backing is common. Clashes between supporters of rival political parties and their student and youth wings and even factions within the same party are frequent occurrences. General strikes and blockades called by political parties mostly affect businesses by keeping workers away with the threat of violence and blocking transport, resulting in productivity losses. Vehicles and other property are at risk from vandalism or arson during such programs, and looting of shops has occurred.

Responding to public concern over law and order, the government in March 2004 created a special elite force, known as the Rapid Action Battalion (RAB) as part of its anti-crime initiative. The RAB is comprised of members of the armed forces, the police, and the Bangladesh Border Guard and Ansars, both paramilitary groups. The RAB became operational in June 2004 and has been credited by many Bangladeshis with improving domestic law and order. Soon after its formation, however, the local media began reporting on "cross-fires," a euphemism for extrajudicial killings, particularly by the RAB.

In February 2005 the government banned two extremist groups: Jama'atul Mujahedin Bangladesh (JMB) and Jagroto Muslim Janata Bangladesh (JMJB). On August 17, 2005, JMB, with the assistance of JMJB, set off over 500 small, improvised explosive devices (IEDs) in a coordinated attack in 63 of the 64 districts of Bangladesh. The devices were accompanied by leaflets demanding the establishment of Islamic law in Bangladesh. From September to early December 2005, JMB conducted several suicide attacks targeting local judges, courts and district government facilities. The government responded vigorously, arresting several high-ranking leaders of JMB and recovering detonators, explosives and related materials used to construct IEDs. As of January 2013, there had been no attacks by extremist groups on foreign diplomatic, commercial or social interests in Bangladesh; the current Awami League government has demonstrated a strong commitment to combating terrorism.

CORRUPTION

Bangladesh has made some progress in reducing corruption during the last decade, but it remains a serious impediment to investment and economic growth in Bangladesh. While the Government has established legislation to combat bribery, embezzlement and other forms of corruption, enforcement is inconsistent. The 2007-2008 Caretaker Government attempted to address the culture of impunity that existed in Bangladesh by prosecuting corruption cases, implementing systemic reforms, and strengthening the Anti-Corruption Commission (ACC) as the main institutional anti-corruption watchdog. The Caretaker Government also took steps to improve administrative efficiency in public services such as law enforcement agencies, power generation and distribution, ports, and customs. The current Awami League-led government has publicly underscored its commitment to anti-corruption efforts and reaffirmed the need for a strong ACC. However, efforts to ease public procurement rules and proposals to curb the independence of the ACC may undermine institutional safeguards against corruption. Bangladesh is a party to the UN Anticorruption Convention, but has not joined the OECD Convention on Combating Bribery of Public Officials.

Corruption is common in public procurement, tax and customs collection, and regulatory authorities. Corruption, including bribery, raises the costs and risks of doing business. By some estimates, off-the-record payments by firms may result in an annual reduction of 2%–3% of GDP. Corruption has a corrosive impact on the broader business climate market and opportunities for U.S. companies in Bangladesh. It also deters investment, stifles economic growth and development, distorts prices, and undermines the rule of law.

ANTI-CORRUPTION RESOURCES

Some useful resources for individuals and companies regarding combating corruption in global markets include the following:

- Information about the U.S. Foreign Corrupt Practices Act (FCPA), including a "Lay-Person's Guide to the FCPA", is available at the U.S. Department of Justice's Website at: http://www.justice.gov/criminal/fraud/fcpa.
- UN Convention: The UN Anticorruption Convention entered into force on December 14, 2005, and there are 143 parties to it as of December 2009 (see http://www.unodc.org/unodc/en/treaties/CAC/signatories.html). The UN Convention is the first global comprehensive international anticorruption agreement. The UN Convention requires countries to establish criminal and other offenses to cover a wide range of acts of corruption, ranging from basic forms of corruption such as bribery and solicitation, embezzlement and trading in influence to the concealment and laundering of the proceeds of corruption.
- Information about the OECD Anti-bribery Convention, including links to national implementing legislation and country monitoring reports, is available at: http://www.oecd.org/department/0,3355,en_2649_34859_1_1_1_1_1,00.html. See also new Anti-bribery Recommendation and Good Practice Guidance Annex for companies: http://www.oecd.org/dataoecd/11/40/44176910.pdf.
- Transparency International (TI) publishes an annual Corruption Perceptions Index (CPI). The CPI measures the perceived level of public-sector corruption in 180 countries and territories around the world. The CPI is available at: http://www.transparency.org/policy_research/surveys_indices/cpi/2009. TI also publishes an annual Global Corruption Report, which provides a systematic evaluation of the state of corruption around the world. It includes an in-depth analysis of a focal theme, a series of country reports that document major

corruption related events and developments from all continents, and an overview of the latest research findings on anti-corruption diagnostics and tools. See http://www.transparency.org/publications/gcr.

- The World Bank Institute publishes Worldwide Governance Indicators (WGI). These indicators assess six dimensions of governance in 212 countries, including Voice and Accountability, Political Stability and Absence of Violence, Government Effectiveness, Regulatory Quality, Rule of Law, and Control of Corruption. See http://info.worldbank.org/governance/wgi/sc_country.asp. The World Bank Business Environment and Enterprise Performance Surveys may also be of interest and are available at: http://go.worldbank.org/RQQXYJ6210.

Bilateral Investment Agreements

The U.S.-Bangladesh Bilateral Investment Treaty, signed on March 12, 1986, entered into force on July 23, 1989. Bangladesh has also signed investment treaties with Austria, Belgium, Canada, China, Democratic People's Republic of Korea, France, Germany, Indonesia, Iran, Italy, Japan, Malaysia, Pakistan, Philippines, Poland, Republic of Korea, Romania, Switzerland, Thailand, The Netherlands, Turkey, Uzbekistan and the United Kingdom. The Foreign Investment Act includes a guarantee of national treatment.

A bilateral treaty between the United States and Bangladesh for the avoidance of double taxation was signed on September 26, 2004 and ratified by the United States on March 31, 2006. The parties exchanged Instruments of ratification on August 7, 2006. The treaty has been effective for most taxpayers beginning in their 2007 tax year.

From 2001-2010, Bangladesh has successfully negotiated several regional trade and economic agreements, including the South Asian Free Trade Area (SAFTA), the Asia-Pacific Trade Agreement (APTA), and the Bay of Bengal Initiative for Multi-Sectoral, Technical and Economic Cooperation (BIMSTEC). Bangladesh has taken steps to strengthen bilateral economic relations with India by reducing trade barriers and improving connectivity. India lifted almost all tariffs on Bangladeshi exports in 2011 and the countries are working to reduce non-tariff barriers. As a founding member of the WTO and as a Least-Developed Country (LDC), Bangladesh has been an active advocate for LDC interests in WTO negotiations.

OPIC and Other Investment Insurance Programs

The U.S. Overseas Private Investment Corporation (OPIC) provides insurance coverage for some U.S. firms currently doing business in Bangladesh. OPIC and the GOB signed an updated bilateral agreement in May 1998. More information on OPIC services can be found on www.opic.gov. Bangladesh is a member of the Multilateral Investment Guarantee Agency.

Labor

Bangladesh has a population of about 155 million people and a labor force of 57 million people, including 2.5 million union members, with 63% working in the agricultural sector, 11% in industry, and the remaining 26% in the services sector. Low official unemployment statistics obscure a huge and growing under-employment problem in Bangladesh. Bangladesh's comparative advantage in cheap labor for manufacturing is partially offset by low productivity due to low skills, poor management, and inefficient infrastructure and machinery.

Bangladesh has labor laws that specify employment conditions, working hours, minimum wage levels, leave policies, health and sanitary conditions, and compensation for injured workers. Freedom of association and the right to join unions are guaranteed in the Bangladesh Constitution. In practice, compliance and enforcement of labor laws are inconsistent, and companies frequently discourage the formation of active labor unions. Historically, unions are heavily politicized, and labor-management relations are often contentious, particularly in the ready-made garment sector which has over 141 registered trade unions.

In July 2004, the Bangladesh parliament enacted a law granting limited freedom of association in the export processing zones. Workers of the industrial units are allowed to form a welfare council to develop and grow into organizations, defending their welfare through collective bargaining, according to the law which was renewed and updated in 2010. These special labor provisions for export processing zones are due to expire in 2013. The implementation of workers' welfare councils in the export processing zones is uneven with many larger factories ignoring the provision altogether. Labor disputes do not necessarily need to be heard before a court. Many companies have found it effective to resolve issues before a Labor Tribunal.

Child Labor

Bangladeshi law sets a minimum age of 14 for employment and 18 for hazardous work. Numerous laws prohibit child labor in certain sectors, ranging from transport workers to tea plantation labor, but these have not been consistently applied to informal sectors, such as agriculture and domestic work, where the majority of children are employed. As a result, child labor in Bangladesh has historically been a fact of life. On July 4, 1995, Bangladesh's garment exporters association signed a memorandum of understanding (MOU) with the United Nations Children's Fund (UNICEF) and the International Labor Organization (ILO) under which child laborers in the EPZ textile factories were removed and enrolled in education programs. ILO-assisted monitoring teams, which found child laborers in 43% of EPZ factories in 1996, found them in fewer than 5% in 2001. The MOU program has been phased out, and the U.S. Embassy considers the project a success, with most child labor now eradicated from the EPZs. Child labor laws are not effectively enforced outside of the EPZs, particularly in the informal sector that employs 80 percent of the workforce. Bangladesh, however, is working to improve compliance with ILO conventions on child labor.

In response to a petition from U.S. labor groups, the office of the U.S. Trade Representative (USTR) is reviewing labor practices in Bangladesh to determine whether insufficient enforcement of labor rights could disqualify Bangladesh from eligibility for preferential U.S. market access under the Generalized System of Preferences (GSP).

The International Labor Organization, in partnership with the International Finance Corporation, plans to initiate a Better Work program in Bangladesh in early-2013 once the GOB establishes an enabling environment to ensure the program's success, including needed labor law reforms and an effective process for union registrations. The program will be similar to Better Factories Cambodia, which was established in 2001, but on a much larger scale to include as many as 500 of Bangladesh's ready-made garment factories.

Foreign Trade Zones/Free Ports

Under the Bangladesh Export Processing Zones Authority Act of 1980, the government established an EPZ in Chittagong in 1983. Additional EPZs now operate in Dhaka (Savar), Mongla, Ishwardi, Comilla, Uttara, Karnaphuli (Chittagong) and Adamjee (Dhaka). Korean investors are developing a private EPZ in Chittagong. Investments that are 100% foreign-owned, joint ventures and 100% Bangladeshi-owned companies are all permitted to operate and enjoy equal treatment in the EPZs. Approximately a dozen U.S. firms - mostly textile producers - are currently operating in Bangladesh EPZs. Investors are generally satisfied with the operation of Bangladesh's EPZs, which have played a significant role in the success of Bangladesh’s ready-made garment industry.

In 2010, Bangladesh enacted a Special Economic Zone law that allows the creation of privately-owned Special Economic Zones (SEZs) that can produce for export and domestic markets. The International Finance Corporation is assisting the government to establish a Special Economic Zone Authority, modeled after BEPZA, to implement the new law and oversee the establishment of SEZs.

Foreign Direct Investment Inflows

Year	Amount in US $ million
2012	1,130
2011	913
2010	700
2009	1,086
2008	666
Year	Amount in US $ million
2007	792
2006	845

Sources: UNCTAD, World Investment Report 2012.

Foreign Direct Investment Statistics

According to the United Nations Conference on Trade and Development (UNCTAD) World Investment Report 2012, total inward foreign direct investment to Bangladesh was $1.13 billion in 2012, a 24% increase from $913 million in 2011. Outward foreign direct investment flows were negligible. UNCTAD estimated the stock of inward foreign direct investment was $6.7 billion in 2010. Major sources of investment include the U.S., the United Kingdom, South Korea, Japan, Norway and India.

INDEX

A

abolition, 29, 36
abuse, 10, 43, 45, 56, 62, 65, 66, 67, 72, 74, 75, 82, 85
access, ix, 14, 15, 23, 44, 46, 49, 51, 54, 57, 60, 64, 65, 66, 69, 76, 83, 99, 105
accessibility, 68, 69
accounting, 27, 95
ACF, 57, 61
acid, 64
adaptation, 5
administrative efficiency, 101
adults, 44, 75
adverse effects, 16
advertisements, 51
advocacy, 68
age, 27, 43, 62, 66, 67, 68, 76, 105
agencies, 43, 45, 48, 61, 69, 70, 91, 98, 101
agricultural sector, 99, 104
agriculture, 4, 10, 27, 95, 105
AIDS, 6, 72
Al Qaeda, 12
annual review, 33
apparel industry, ix, 4, 23, 36
apparel products, 24
appointments, 47, 60, 94
arbitration, 72, 73
armed conflict, 37, 54
armed forces, 45, 100
arrest(s), x, 40, 41, 43, 45, 46, 48, 52, 53, 61, 63
arson, xi, 48, 80, 85, 100
ASEAN, 14
Asia, vii, viii, xii, 1, 10, 13, 14, 19, 20, 21, 89, 94, 103
assault, 47, 56, 71
assessment, 34, 48, 60
assets, 59, 94, 95, 99
Association of Southeast Asian Nations, 14
asylum, 54, 55
atheists, 12
atrocities, viii, 2
audit(s), 95, 99
Austria, 103
authority(ies), viii, x, 2, 6, 37, 39, 41, 45, 46, 48, 51, 52, 53, 60, 62, 69, 71, 81, 82, 84, 91, 101
autism, 69
autonomy, 99
avoidance, 103
awareness, 13, 64, 69, 71

B

bail, 46, 60, 64
balance of payments, 92
balance sheet, 95
ban, 51, 52, 53, 54, 81
banking, 94, 99

banking sector, 99
banks, 92, 95, 99
bargaining, x, 29, 40, 53, 73, 74, 75, 104
barriers, 64, 66, 103
base, 86, 99
basic raw materials, 95
basic services, 57
Bay of Bengal, vii, 1, 4, 16, 21, 27, 103
Beijing, 20
Belgium, 103
benefits, 11, 27, 30, 36, 77, 91
bilateral, 93, 95, 103
biodiversity, 6, 18
births, 64
blockades, viii, 2, 7, 100
bonds, 27
bonuses, 73
bounds, 96
Brazil, 3
bribes, 47
building code, 26
Burma, 7, 8, 13, 14, 25, 27, 33, 55, 56, 57
businesses, xii, 30, 31, 34, 90, 97, 98, 100
buyer, 31
buyers, 4, 33, 64, 75

C

Cambodia, 29, 105
capital account, 93
capital gains, 93
capital markets, 98
caregivers, 68
cash, 60
censorship, x, 40, 51, 61
Census, 21
central bank, 93
challenges, viii, 2, 17
chemicals, 76, 78
Chief of Staff, 11
child abuse, 66
child development, 69
child labor, 29, 30, 36, 76, 77, 78, 105
children, x, 6, 8, 27, 30, 37, 40, 56, 62, 63, 64, 65, 66, 67, 68, 76, 77, 105
China, viii, 2, 3, 4, 13, 14, 15, 20, 27, 103
Christians, 80, 81
CIA, 27
city(ies), 8, 80, 85
citizens, x, 7, 40, 44, 48, 49, 53, 57, 58, 66, 78, 81
citizenship, 57, 66
civil servants, 98
civil service, 70, 97
civil society, x, xi, 33, 40, 59, 80, 86, 90
classes, 82
clients, 46, 95
climate, vii, viii, 2, 5, 16, 17, 45, 98, 102
climate change, viii, 2, 5, 16, 17
CNN, 12, 20
coal, 90
Coast Guard, 4
codes of conduct, ix, 24, 26, 29, 30, 36, 37
coercion, 64
collaboration, 3
collateral, 95
collective bargaining, x, 29, 40, 53, 73, 74, 75, 104
colleges, 69
collusion, 41, 50
commerce, 93, 97
commercial, 67, 73, 92, 99, 101
commercial bank, 92, 99
commercial sexual exploitation of children, 67
community(ies), xi, 6, 7, 9, 17, 36, 45, 54, 57, 66, 68, 69, 70, 71, 72, 80, 81, 84, 85, 86, 87, 89, 97, 98, 100
comparative advantage, 104
compensation, 47, 62, 94, 104
competition, 92
competitiveness, 92
compliance, 50, 69, 97, 104, 105
computer, 96
conciliation, 73
conference, 33
confidentiality, 71, 97
conflict, 12, 37, 54, 84
Congress, ix, 1, 9, 23, 24, 31, 35, 36
connectivity, 4, 14, 90, 92, 103

consent, 67, 73, 81, 82
conservation, 6, 17
conspiracy, 61
Constitution, 104
construction, 10, 11, 69, 76, 85
consumer goods, 97
consumers, 4, 100
consumption, 4
conviction, 64
cooperation, vii, viii, 1, 4, 11, 14, 15
copyright, 97
Corporate Social Responsibility (CSR), 100
corruption, vii, viii, x, xii, 1, 2, 3, 11, 27, 40, 45, 46, 47, 50, 59, 60, 90, 94, 101, 102
cost, 37, 97
cotton, 27
counsel, 47
counterterrorism, 3, 12
Coup, 20
CPI, 102
cracks, ix, 23, 24
credit market, 99
crimes, viii, 2, 8, 46, 47, 54
criminal activity, 45, 46
criminal gangs, 41
criminals, 44
crisis management, 74
criticism, 5, 49, 51, 61
crop, 17
culture, ix, 24, 70, 101
currency, 92, 93
current account, 92, 93
curricula, 13
curriculum, 13, 82, 83
cyclones, 17

D

death penalty, 12
deaths, viii, x, 4, 7, 11, 23, 40, 41, 43, 64, 70
debts, 65, 99
defamation, 49, 51
defendants, 46, 47
deficiency, 68
deficit, 92
degradation, 17
Delta, 27
democracy, vii, ix, 1, 2, 3, 6, 11, 13, 27, 39, 54, 87
democratic government, viii, 2
demonstrations, viii, xii, 2, 7, 46, 52, 74, 90
denial, 8, 73
Department of Commerce, 27
Department of Defense, 3
Department of Justice, 102
Department of Labor, ix, 24, 33, 77
deployments, 83
depreciation, 92, 96
deprivation, 56
depth, 102
destruction, 74, 86
detainees, 44, 46
detection, 4, 12
detention, 45, 46, 56
developing countries, ix, 23, 24, 29
developing nations, 3
development assistance, 6, 9
development banks, 95
direct investment, xii, 27, 89, 106
disability, 68
disaster, 3, 5, 12, 15, 24, 33, 66
disaster relief, 3
discrimination, x, xi, 7, 29, 36, 39, 62, 64, 68, 69, 70, 72, 73, 80, 84, 91
diseases, 4
dissatisfaction, 60
distortions, 98
distribution, 92, 101
diversity, 87
domestic investment, 98
domestic markets, 106
domestic violence, 44, 63
donors, 60
draft, 15, 97, 98
drinking water, 16
drug trafficking, 37
drugs, 76
drying, 76
due process, xi, 80

dyeing, 76

E

earnings, 96
East Asia, xii, 90
Easter, 83
e-commerce, 93
economic assistance, vii, viii, 1
economic cooperation, 4
economic development, 3, 30
economic disadvantage, 62
economic growth, 3, 10, 18, 94, 98, 101, 102
economic leverage, 15
economic migrants, 55, 57
economic reform(s), 27
economic relations, 103
economic resources, 17
education, 9, 10, 12, 56, 57, 64, 65, 66, 68, 69, 70, 77, 84, 105
educational attainment, 9
educational institutions, 64
election, 7, 59
electricity, 15
embassy, xi, 13, 80, 86, 87
emergency, 56, 78
emigration, 54
employees, 31, 68, 72, 74, 83
employers, 26, 72, 73, 75, 76, 77
employment, 10, 27, 29, 30, 36, 37, 65, 68, 69, 75, 76, 78, 104, 105
empowerment, 9, 10
energy, xi, 3, 4, 14, 89, 92, 96, 98, 99
enforcement, xii, 4, 27, 29, 41, 42, 43, 45, 46, 47, 48, 53, 62, 64, 65, 68, 69, 70, 76, 77, 78, 83, 85, 86, 90, 95, 101, 104, 105
environment(s), ix, 5, 8, 24, 105
environmental change, 17
environmental degradation, 17
environmental protection, 15
environmental sustainability, 17
equality, 10, 13, 87
equipment, 4, 91, 96
equity, 11
ethnic groups, xi, 70, 80
ethnic minority, 80
Europe, 4, 26, 31, 35
European Union, 24
evacuation, 25, 78
evidence, 47, 60
examinations, 57, 69
exchange rate, 93
execution, 97
executive branch, 47
exercise, ix, 23, 73
expertise, 63, 84
exploitation, 67, 76
explosives, 101
export market, 27, 37
exporters, 91, 105
export-led growth, xii, 90
exports, 16, 25, 27, 30, 95, 103
exposure, 78
extraction, 96
extremists, viii, 2, 9, 20, 83

F

Facebook, 49, 51, 84, 85
factories, ix, x, 5, 10, 24, 25, 30, 34, 35, 37, 39, 65, 73, 74, 75, 78, 105
fairness, 48
faith, 35, 86
families, 10, 26, 54, 66, 77, 84, 85
family law, xi, 79, 81
family members, 11
family planning, 6, 13, 64
fatwa, 63, 84
fear(s), 30, 45, 51, 52, 62
female prisoners, 44
films, 51
financial, xii, 16, 82, 89, 92, 98
financial markets, 98
fire hazard, 26, 31
fires, 100
fish, 76
floods, 17
flowers, 76
foils, 20

food, viii, 2, 17, 56, 74
food production, 17
food security, viii, 2
force, x, xi, 7, 27, 30, 40, 45, 52, 55, 60, 73, 82, 89, 93, 100, 102, 103, 104
foreign assistance, ix, 24
foreign direct investment, xii, 27, 89, 106
foreign exchange, 16, 92, 93
foreign firms, 93
foreign investment, xi, xii, 73, 89, 91, 98
formal sector, 10
formation, 74, 100, 104
France, 103
fraud, 8, 55, 75, 102
free trade, ix, 24, 37
freedom, vii, x, 29, 36, 40, 49, 51, 52, 54, 56, 68, 79, 81, 83, 84, 86, 104
friendship, 27
funding, 53, 84, 90
funds, 5, 84, 93

G

gangs, 41
garment factory, viii, 10, 23, 65
garment industry, 9, 10, 24, 31, 33, 73, 74, 77, 106
GDP, 15, 27, 101
gender equality, 13, 87
gender equity, 11
Generalized System of Preferences, 4, 27, 29, 37, 105
geography, 16
geopolitical, vii, viii, 1, 13
George Mitchell, 35
Germany, 103
global demand, 26
global markets, 102
globalization, 30
GNP, 16
God, 20
governance, viii, 2, 3, 4, 18, 87, 103
governments, xii, 10, 11, 17, 26, 90
grants, 11
green revolution, 17
gross domestic product, 2
growth, xi, xii, 3, 10, 15, 18, 27, 89, 90, 94, 98, 99, 101, 102
growth rate, 27
guardian, 10
guidelines, 99, 100
guilty, 41

H

Haiti, 29
harassment, xi, 49, 50, 62, 64, 65, 80, 85, 86
harmful effects, 10
harmony, 13, 85
hazards, 26, 33
health, ix, 6, 9, 10, 17, 24, 27, 29, 30, 37, 57, 65, 69, 78, 104
health care, 57
health risks, 10
health services, 57
health status, 6
height, 66
hemorrhage, 64
high school, 57, 85
higher education, 70
Hindus, xi, 9, 48, 79, 80, 81, 82, 83, 85
hiring, 35, 62, 83
history, ix, 4, 23, 24, 52
HIV, 6, 72
HIV/AIDS, 6, 72
homes, xi, 48, 56, 63, 69, 70, 80, 85, 86
host, 57
House, 31, 32, 37
human, vii, x, 1, 3, 7, 8, 13, 27, 39, 40, 41, 44, 45, 47, 48, 51, 52, 53, 54, 56, 60, 61, 62, 66, 71, 72, 75, 87
human right(s), vii, x, 1, 3, 7, 13, 27, 39, 40, 41, 44, 45, 48, 51, 53, 54, 56, 60, 61, 62, 66, 71, 72, 87
humanitarian organizations, 54
husband, 11, 63, 65, 82

I

ICC, 62
identity, 11, 26, 42, 50
ideology, 4
immigrants, 8, 15
import sensitive, 30
import substitution, 95
imports, 17, 27, 30, 91, 92
imprisonment, 44, 49, 67, 75, 76
improvements, 5, 35
income, 2, 7, 16, 50, 59, 64, 77, 96
income tax, 50, 96
independence, viii, 2, 8, 9, 11, 15, 26, 27, 47, 51, 52, 94, 101
India, viii, 2, 3, 4, 8, 9, 10, 13, 14, 15, 17, 20, 21, 25, 27, 103, 107
individuals, x, 7, 40, 48, 56, 59, 60, 64, 70, 71, 81, 102
Indonesia, 103
industrial policy(ies), xi, 89, 95
industry(ies), viii, ix, xi, 2, 4, 5, 9, 10, 23, 24, 26, 27, 31, 33, 34, 36, 53, 67, 73, 74, 76, 77, 78, 89, 91, 94, 95, 96, 97, 104, 106
inequity, 10
inflation, 34, 74, 77, 98
informal sector, x, 40, 67, 76, 78, 105
information technology, xi, 89, 98
infrastructure, xi, xii, 6, 15, 27, 89, 90, 91, 92, 104
inheritance, 65
injuries, 70, 78
inmates, 46
innocence, 60
insecticide, 96
inspections, 5, 35
inspectors, 27, 33, 34, 35, 78
institutions, 59, 64, 66, 83
integration, 4, 57
integrity, 34
intellectual property, 16, 97
intellectual property rights, 97
intelligence, 48, 51, 61, 70
interest groups, 30
interference, 48, 49, 59, 73
internally displaced, 54
International Development Association (IDA), 99
International Narcotics Control, 6
international organizations, ix, 24
international standards, 56, 62, 95, 99, 100
internationally recognized worker rights, ix, 23, 24, 26, 27, 29, 30
interrogations, 43
intervention, xi, 80
intimidation, 47, 50, 55, 60, 74
investment(s), vii, xi, xii, 3, 14, 15, 16, 17, 27, 73, 89, 90, 91, 92, 93, 94, 95, 96, 98, 101, 102, 103, 107
investment incentive, xi, 89, 98
investors, xi, xii, 3, 10, 35, 89, 90, 91, 94, 95, 98, 99, 106
Iowa, vii, 1, 25, 26, 27
IPR, 97
Iran, 103
iron, 27, 96
Islam, xi, 9, 12, 41, 42, 43, 49, 53, 69, 74, 79, 80, 81, 84
Islamic law, 63, 81, 84, 101
Islamic world, vii, 1, 3
Islamism, 20
Islamist, viii, 2, 7, 8, 9, 11, 12, 15, 20
Israel, 54
issues, ix, 4, 9, 24, 31, 32, 33, 34, 35, 50, 85, 95, 99, 105
Italy, 103

J

Japan, 103, 107
job skills, 71
joint ventures, 106
journalists, x, 9, 40, 42, 49, 50, 71, 85
judiciary, xii, 47, 60, 90, 94
juries, 47
juveniles, 44

K

kidnapping, 66
kill, 11
Korea, 103, 107

L

labor force, xi, 27, 30, 89, 104
land acquisition, 92
landscape, 7
law enforcement, 4, 41, 42, 43, 45, 47, 48, 53, 69, 83, 85, 86, 101
laws, x, 7, 26, 27, 31, 34, 44, 49, 54, 55, 57, 59, 62, 63, 65, 74, 75, 76, 78, 79, 81, 91, 95, 96, 97, 98, 104, 105
lawyers, 46, 55
leadership, 11
Leahy, 37
legal protection, 57
legislation, 54, 65, 72, 97, 98, 101, 102
liberation, xi, 54, 79
liberty, 40
lifetime, 65
light, 10, 34, 76
limited company, 92
literacy, 84
loans, 11, 35, 91, 95, 96
local authorities, 84
local government, 51, 86
lying, vii, 1, 5, 14, 16, 17

M

machinery, 27, 78, 91, 95, 96, 104
mainstream society, 71
majority, vii, viii, xi, 1, 2, 6, 8, 10, 54, 78, 80, 91, 105
Malaysia, 103
malnutrition, 66
man, 81
management, 6, 15, 17, 24, 34, 37, 74, 78, 104
management committee, 74
manipulation, 55
manufacturing, 24, 26, 27, 76, 94, 95, 104
marginalisation, 10
maritime security, 3
market access, 105
market capitalization, 98
marketing, 92
marriage, x, xi, 40, 57, 64, 67, 79, 81, 82
mass, vii, 1, 9, 12, 27, 47, 61
materials, 37, 95, 96, 101
matter, 73
media, 9, 12, 41, 44, 49, 50, 51, 58, 59, 61, 62, 72, 100
mediation, 48
medical, 4, 44, 57, 69
medical care, 44, 57
membership, 72
messages, 13
Middle East, 14, 16
migrants, 55, 57
migration, 10, 56
militancy, viii, 2
military, vii, viii, 1, 3, 4, 9, 11, 12, 47, 55, 70, 83
military-to-military, vii, viii, 1
mineral resources, 92
minimum wage, 27, 30, 34, 77, 78, 104
minimum wages, 27, 30, 77
Ministry of Education, 13
minority(ies), x, xi, 7, 9, 40, 54, 59, 62, 79, 80, 82, 83, 84, 85, 86, 87
minority groups, xi, 7, 62, 80, 83
minors, 44
missions, 4, 53
mobile phone, 91
modernization, 99
monetary policy, 98
morality, xi, 49, 53, 79, 81
mortality, 64
MSF, 57, 61
multilateral, 104
multinational corporations, 26, 30
multinational firms, 100
murder, 47, 48
music, 70

Muslim country, vii, 1
Muslims, 51, 53, 71, 80, 81

N

national character, 87
National Party, viii, 2, 6
National Retail Federation, 35
national security, 14, 46, 60
nationalism, 11
nationalists, 8
nationality, 57
natural gas, 16, 92
natural resource management, 6
natural resources, 18
neglect, 82
Netherlands, 103
NGOs, x, 40, 51, 53, 57, 61, 63, 65, 67, 69, 70, 72, 74, 75, 82, 86
North America, 5, 19, 38
Norway, 107
nutrition, 6, 10, 56, 65

O

Obama, 3, 4, 31
Obama Administration, 3
obstacles, x, 40, 86
obstruction, 97
occupational health, 78
OECD, 100, 101, 102
offenders, 44, 64
officials, x, xi, 7, 8, 9, 29, 34, 35, 40, 41, 42, 44, 47, 50, 53, 54, 59, 60, 61, 70, 74, 79, 80, 85, 86, 87, 97, 98
oil, 100
operations, 3, 4, 24, 26, 27, 41, 57, 59, 76
opportunities, xi, 65, 89, 98, 102
opposition parties, 45, 48, 58, 60
organize, ix, 23, 27, 30, 36, 58, 74
outreach, 61
overlap, 80
Overseas Private Investment Corporation, 104
oversight, 13, 35, 37, 68, 76, 98
overtime, 73, 77
ownership, 60, 81, 91, 94, 95

P

Pacific, 3, 19, 103
Pakistan, vii, viii, 1, 2, 8, 9, 13, 15, 20, 27, 103
parents, 66, 67
parity, 11, 27
Parliament, 34, 36
peace, vii, viii, 1, 3, 4, 14, 15, 70
peacekeeping, vii, viii, 1, 3, 4
penalties, 59, 62, 76
Pentagon, 20
per capita income, 16
percentile, 93
permission, 48, 56, 57, 81
permit, 34, 44
perpetrators, 42, 69, 70
Persian Gulf, 10
persons with disabilities, x, 40, 62, 68, 69
petroleum, 92
pharmaceutical(s), xi, 89, 96
Philippines, 103
photographs, 51
Poland, 103
police, xi, 4, 25, 41, 42, 43, 45, 46, 48, 49, 50, 52, 60, 62, 63, 64, 66, 69, 71, 72, 74, 79, 85, 86, 94, 100
policy, vii, xi, 1, 3, 14, 18, 55, 89, 90, 93, 98, 102
political affiliations, 52
political instability, 27
political leaders, 8
political parties, 6, 7, 59, 74, 97, 100
political party, 8, 47
political recourse, xi, 80, 85
political uncertainty, xii, 90
politics, viii, 2, 81
polygamy, 81, 82
population, vii, viii, xi, 1, 2, 9, 16, 17, 25, 26, 27, 44, 49, 55, 57, 68, 80, 83, 104
population density, 17

population growth, 16
portfolio, 60, 98
portfolio investment, 98
poverty, viii, 2, 8, 9, 10, 27, 65, 77
poverty line, 27
power generation, 90, 92, 99, 101
precedent, 75
president, 4, 30, 31, 50
President Obama, 4, 31
presidential authority, 37
prevention, 6, 12, 68
primary school, 13, 66, 82
primary school enrollment, 66
principles, 11, 26, 29, 36, 37, 81
prisoners, 44, 46
prisons, 44
private banks, 99
private investment, 92
private sector, ix, 24, 29, 31, 34, 75, 94, 97, 98
private sector employers, 75
privatization, 97
procurement, 90, 101
producers, 91, 106
professionalism, 45
professionals, 9, 97
profit, 95
programming, 49
progress reports, 5
project, 5, 11, 13, 15, 17, 59, 61, 71, 90, 99, 105
property rights, 97
proposed regulations, 98
prosperity, 3
protection, 8, 15, 27, 30, 54, 55, 56, 57, 66, 72, 82, 97
protectionism, 97
public awareness, 13
public concern, 100
public education, 68
public health, 57
public limited company, 92
public officials, 61
public safety, 52
public schools, 57
public service, 101
public television, 49
publishing, 50, 61
punishment, 41, 43, 63, 66, 70, 73, 84
purchasing power, 27
purchasing power parity, 27

Q

quotas, 70

R

radicalism, 12
radicals, 12
radio, 49
rape, 43, 44, 56, 62, 66
rapists, 62
ratification, 103
raw materials, 95, 96
real property, 95, 96
recognition, 29
recommendations, 10, 70
reconstruction, 85
reform(s), 7, 33, 38
reforms, 10, 27, 97, 101, 105
refugee camps, 55, 56
refugee status, 55, 56
refugees, x, 7, 8, 39, 53, 54, 55, 56, 57, 61, 80
regional integration, 4
regulations, 74, 75, 78, 91, 93, 97, 98
regulatory framework, 90
regulatory oversight, 98
rehabilitation, 68, 69
relief, 3, 4, 86
religion, xi, 53, 79, 81, 82, 84
religious belief(s), x, xi, 40, 80, 81, 82, 83
remittances, 10, 15, 16, 94
renewable energy, 3
rent, 98
repatriate, 93
repression, 74
reputation, vii, 1, 26, 31, 35, 94

requirements, 27, 29, 58, 61, 69, 73, 90, 91, 97, 99
researchers, 78
reserves, 4, 16, 92, 94
resettlement, 55
resilience, viii, 2
resistance, 97
resolution, xii, 48, 73, 81, 90, 94
resource management, 6
resources, 14, 15, 17, 18, 46, 65, 90, 92, 97, 102
response, 12, 29, 34, 35, 50, 105
responsiveness, 45
restoration, 52
restrictions, x, 40, 51, 53, 57, 61, 63, 64, 72, 82, 84, 99
retail, 35, 98
retirement, 34
retribution, 45, 51
revenue, 16, 51, 91, 95
right to life, 40
risk(s), xii, 10, 37, 83, 90, 92, 98, 100, 101
risk management, 37
Romania, 103
routes, ix, 4, 13, 23
rule of law, x, 7, 40, 102
rules, 46, 73, 101
rural areas, 75, 82
rural poverty, 9
Russia, 3, 11, 16, 20

S

safe haven(s), 12
safety, viii, ix, x, 2, 5, 10, 24, 25, 27, 29, 30, 33, 34, 35, 36, 37, 39, 52, 78
salinity, 17
scarcity, 91, 92
school, x, 13, 40, 57, 66, 67, 68, 76, 82, 83, 85, 86
school enrollment, 66
science, 13
sea level, 16, 17
secondary school students, 83
security, viii, x, 2, 3, 4, 7, 8, 14, 39, 40, 41, 42, 43, 45, 46, 49, 50, 51, 54, 60, 70, 72, 73, 74, 83, 85, 96
security assistance, 3
security forces, x, 8, 39, 40, 43, 45, 54, 73, 74, 85
security guard, 72
security services, x, 39, 42
self-monitoring, 32
self-sufficiency, 17
seminars, 70
Senate, 32, 35
sentencing, 44
services, x, 27, 39, 42, 55, 57, 69, 76, 98, 101, 104
sex, 37, 67, 71, 72
sexual abuse, 43, 66, 75
sexual activity, 71
sexual harassment, 64, 65
sexual orientation, x, 40, 71
shareholders, 100
shelter, 56, 63, 76
shock, 43
showing, 42
shrimp, 53, 76, 78
signs, 74
skills training, 68, 71
smuggling, 56, 76
social development, 82
social hierarchy, 85
social interests, 101
social responsibility, ix, 24
social status, xi, 80
societal violence, x, 40, 45, 70
society, x, xi, 8, 33, 40, 59, 71, 80, 86, 90
socio-religious prejudices, viii, 2
soft loan, 99
software, 97
solidarity, 71
solution, 74
South Asia, vii, viii, xii, 1, 12, 13, 14, 20, 21, 89, 94, 103
South Korea, 107
Southeast Asia, 14
Spain, 35

specialists, 68
speculation, 93
speech, x, 40, 49
Spring, 21
Sri Lanka, 9, 15, 19
stability, vii, xii, 1, 3, 7, 14, 90
stakeholders, 31, 33
standard of living, 26, 77
state(s), xi, 4, 6, 13, 14, 46, 49, 50, 51, 53, 59, 68, 76, 79, 81, 82, 83, 92, 95, 99, 100, 102
state-owned banks, 99
state-owned enterprises, 92
statistics, 40, 67, 78, 83, 104
steel, 27, 91, 96
stigma, 62, 71
stock, 98, 107
stress, 66
structure, ix, 24, 26, 70, 71, 95
substitution, 95
suicide, 63, 66, 101
suicide attacks, 101
supplier(s), 4, 31
supply chain, viii, ix, 2, 24
support staff, 62
Supreme Court, 50, 58, 63, 64, 81, 84
surplus, 92
surveillance, 48, 71
survival, 9
survivors, 66
sustainability, 17
sustainable development, 21, 17
Switzerland, 103

T

tariff, 27, 29, 36, 37, 38, 95, 103
tax evasion, 50
tax incentive, 91, 96
taxation, 103
taxes, 50, 69, 91, 97
taxpayers, 103
teachers, 13, 52, 68, 87
teams, 105
technical assistance, ix, 24, 29, 99
technology(ies), xi, 17, 89, 98
technology transfer, 17
telecommunications, 92, 98
Telecommunications Act, 91
temperature, 17
temporary protection, 55
tension(s), 10, 17, 52, 85
terrorism, 12, 101
terrorist attack, 12
terrorist groups, 11, 12
terrorists, 12, 15
textbooks, 52
textiles, xi, 25, 27, 89
Thailand, 103
threats, 43, 50, 61, 75
threshold level, 56
torture, 41, 43, 74, 81
trade, ix, 3, 4, 13, 14, 16, 24, 26, 29, 37, 53, 56, 64, 72, 73, 93, 95, 97, 103, 104
trade agreement, ix, 24, 37
Trade Policy Staff Committee, 33
trade preference, ix, 24, 26, 29
trade union, 53, 72, 73, 97, 104
traditions, 70
trafficking, x, 7, 8, 37, 40, 44, 66, 75
training, 5, 12, 13, 45, 60, 61, 68, 71, 84, 87
transactions, 93, 95, 96
transmission, 51
transparency, 62, 90, 97, 102
transport, viii, 2, 7, 45, 68, 76, 100, 105
transportation, 14, 99
treaties, 102, 103
treatment, x, 37, 38, 39, 43, 54, 58, 68, 86, 98, 103, 106
trial, 44, 45, 46, 47, 61
tuberculosis, 6
Turkey, 103

U

U.S. assistance, 3, 5
U.S. policy, vii, 1, 3
UNDP, 9
unemployment rate, 27, 78
UNHCR, 54, 55, 56, 57

unions, x, 31, 34, 39, 53, 72, 73, 74, 75, 78, 81, 97, 104
United Kingdom, 103, 107
United Nations (UN), 3, 4, 19, 20, 54, 61, 63, 67, 94, 101, 102, 105, 106
United Nations Development Program(me), 19, 20
United States, vii, 1, 2, 3, 4, 12, 14, 16, 25, 26, 27, 30, 31, 37, 103
universities, 85
urban, 56, 75, 76, 77, 83
urban areas, 75, 76, 83
Uzbekistan, 103

V

vandalism, 100
varieties, 17
vehicles, 25
ventilation, 44
vested interests, 97
victims, xi, 9, 43, 44, 60, 62, 63, 64, 66, 67, 71, 72, 76, 80
violence, viii, x, xi, 2, 7, 8, 9, 39, 40, 41, 42, 44, 45, 52, 55, 56, 62, 63, 64, 69, 70, 71, 72, 80, 85, 86, 100
violent extremist, 13
vocational rehabilitation, 69
volatility, 98
voting, 59
vulnerability, 3, 10

W

wage level, 77, 104
wage structure, 77
wages, 10, 27, 30, 34, 65, 73, 74, 75, 77
waiver, 37
war, viii, xi, 2, 8, 9, 13, 27, 47, 54, 79
war crimes, viii, 2, 8, 47, 54
Washington, 38
water, 15, 16, 44, 57
water resources, 15
web, 95
websites, 30
welfare, 34, 65, 75, 104
witnesses, 47
worker rights, viii, ix, 2, 5, 23, 24, 26, 27, 29, 30, 32, 33
workers, ix, 4, 5, 8, 9, 10, 15, 16, 23, 24, 25, 26, 27, 31, 34, 36, 45, 61, 65, 67, 73, 74, 75, 77, 78, 100, 104, 105
workforce, 16, 72, 105
working conditions, ix, x, 7, 24, 26, 27, 32, 39, 78
working hours, 104
workplace, ix, 23, 29, 66, 67
World Bank, 2, 10, 15, 16, 17, 21, 29, 33, 34, 36, 38, 59, 83, 90, 93, 99, 103
World Health Organization, 56
World Trade Organization (WTO), 4, 103
worldwide, 9